Islam
WITHOUT A VEIL

Also by Claude Salhani

Black September to Desert Storm:
A Journalist in the Middle East (1998)

While the Arab World Slept:
The Impact of the Bush Years on the Middle East (2009)

Related Titles from Potomac Books

Simple Gestures:
A Cultural Journey into the Middle East
—Andrea B. Rugh

Fragments of Grace:
My Search for Meaning in the Strife of South Asia
—Pamela Constable

High-Value Target:
Countering al Qaeda in Yemen
—Amb. Edmund J. Hull (Ret.)

Where the Paved Road Ends:
One Woman's Extraordinary Experiences in Yemen
—Carolyn Han

Islam WITHOUT A VEIL

Kazakhstan's
Path of Moderation

CLAUDE SALHANI

Potomac Books
Washington, D.C.

Library of Congress Cataloging-in-Publication Data
Salhani, Claude.
  Islam without a veil : Kazakhstan's path of moderation / Claude Salhani. — 1st ed.
      p. cm.
  Includes bibliographical references and index.
  ISBN 978-1-59797-731-9 (hardcover)
  1. Islam—Kazakhstan. 2. Kazakhstan—Religion. 3. Kazakhstan—Economic conditions—1991– 4. Kazakhstan—Social conditions—1991– I. Title.

  BP63.K3S25 2011
  297.095845—dc22

                                          2011008864

Printed in the United States of America on acid-free paper that meets the American National Standards Institute Z39-48 Standard.

Potomac Books
22841 Quicksilver Drive
Dulles, Virginia 20166

First Edition

10 9 8 7 6 5 4 3 2 1

to my children,
Justin *and* Isabelle,
with much love

CONTENTS

PREFACE

"Islam is a religion that is no better or no worse than other religions."
—*Bulat Sultanov, director, Kazakhstan Institute of Strategic Studies*

The West's curiosity about Islam began in earnest only after the September 11, 2001, terrorist attacks on the United States. To many people it seemed as though this was a declaration of war from the Muslim world on the West. By the vast majority of Westerners, Islam is perceived as a homogeneous, monolithic group. If Muslims were attacking the West it must mean that all Muslims were on the warpath. Right? Nothing could be further from the truth.

All Muslims adore the same God, whose name in Arabic is Allah. All Muslims revere the same prophet, Mohammad,[1] and all Muslims share the same holy book, the Quran.[2] All Muslims believe their holy book was dictated by God to the Prophet and believe that the content of the Quran is the words of God revealed to the Prophet.

But the similarities stop about here because Islam is composed of a number of very different branches that have very different beliefs and approaches to their religion. They are as diverse from one another as are Catholics from Protestants, Orthodox from Lutherans, or Chaldeans from Copts. On the surface Islam may seem a little less complicated, with two main branches, Sunnis and Shiites. But upon closer scrutiny it quickly becomes evident that it is not so clearly cut. Each of the two main branches has several offshoots.

For example, the Druze in Lebanon, Syria, and Israel; the Alaouites in Syria and northern Lebanon; and the Ismailis in Pakistan derive from Shiism; the Wahhabites, from where the *Salafis*[3] and *Takfiris*[4] derive, and who are found mainly in Saudi Arabia; and the Hashemites, after which the Royal Court in Jordan gets its name, are part of Sunni Islam. There are others, of course, such as the Suffis, a mystical offshoot of Islam, but for the purpose of this book we will mainly discuss the Sunni branch of Islam, except when talking about Iran, which is predominantly Shiite.

But it is important to note that there are different tendencies within the different branches. The September 11 attacks did indeed raise the interest in the West about Islam, but most of that interest was centered on the question "Why do they hate us so much?" And the majority of Americans simply placed all Muslims under the same heading. That is far from being the case.

Let us differentiate between regular Muslims—who make up the vast majority of the community, or the Umma, and who we should refer to simply as Muslims—and reserve the word *Islamists* to describe the "fundamentalists." That has been widely accepted as the term referring to people of the Muslim faith who engage in terrorism. That, too, is a generalization as not all fundamentalists and therefore not all Islamists are terrorists, or for that matter anti-Western. To be more precise, there are three names that further differentiate the fundamentalists (though I prefer to use the term "extremists") into at least three very different subgroups: the Muslim Brotherhood, the *Salafis*, and the *Takfiris*. Additionally, it is important to point out that only a small minority, roughly 10 percent of the extreme fringe engage or are willing to engage in acts of terrorism.

Traditionally these three groups have represented the more orthodox and conservative branches of Sunni Islam. They have resisted change on the basis that they believe the religion should be practiced the way it was introduced by the Prophet in his time. And we find major differences between the Muslim Brotherhood, who some see as becoming more moderate, though that remains to be seen, and the *Salafi* and *Takfiri* philosophies.

There is, however, a major difference between *Salafi* and *Takfiri* philosophy. Though ultraconservative, the *Salafis* are reluctant to use violence, whereas the *Takfiris* believe violence should be used as a tool to attain their objectives. *Salafis* are adherents of the Muslim reformer Abd al-Wahab and

are often called Wahhabi, although members of this group prefer to call themselves *Muwahhidun,* meaning unifiers.

We will be talking at greater length about the two groups in the ensuing
pages of this book. But before we do that, it is important to look back at history in order to have a better understanding of the present, and maybe, if we
are not too arrogant to ignore the lessons of history, we just might be able to
preempt the future and avoid repeating the mistakes of the past.

THE CAUCASUS AND CENTRAL ASIA

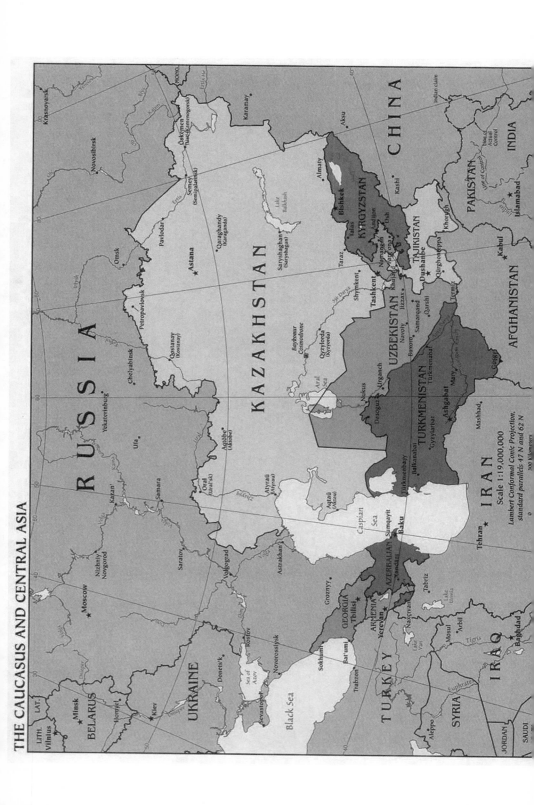

ACKNOWLEDGMENTS

The idea for this book and its title came about as a result of a six-month assignment in Kazakhstan as a correspondent for the *Washington Times* in early 2010. The contents of this work—the words, reflections, comments, analyses, and conclusions—relate to events as I saw them during that time and on follow-up trips to conduct interviews and research for this book. This is the result of intense labor for the good part of a year of continuous reporting and writing.

Most of the research was conducted in Kazakhstan, with side trips to Afghanistan, Kyrgyzstan, and Austria (HQ of the Organization for Security and Cooperation in Europe, OSCE, in Vienna).

This work is based on personal observations and on interviews and conversations with numerous Kazakh and foreign officials, from the highest level of government to lower ranks, and with more than thirty foreign ambassadors based in Astana.

During my brief stay in Astana I was fortunate enough to have been invited to travel with the foreign minister on several of his trips to the surrounding countries in his capacity as chairman of the OSCE. This is a rotating position and Kazakhstan had been awarded the chair for 2010. These trips offered a wonderful insight into the Kazakh government "machine." They allowed me to meet and converse with several of the foreign minister's top advisors, and to get a rare view at the working of this Central Asian country, a young nation in full growth.

If at times I tend to express my support or agreement of actions or policy undertaken by the government of Kazakhstan, it is purely out of my personal conviction that those were the correct steps to take under the circumstances at the time. I often argued with my editors in Washington during my assignment in Astana, who at times disagreed with me. But seen from the ground the story is very different than seen from Washington.

The story, in my opinion—and one I had a hard time impressing upon people back in the United States—was the incredible progress this country that few people in the United States had ever heard of was making in a short time as an independent nation, and the mark it was making on the region. More important, from my perspective, was the manner in which a majority Muslim country such as Kazakhstan could become an example for the rest of the Muslim world to follow—and not only the Muslim world. Thus, the idea of *Islam Without a Veil* was born. I have to admit that I "borrowed" the title from a column I wrote several years ago about Kosovo, where I found a similar attitude toward religion.

In writing this book it is not my intention to promote the Kazakh government's politics or policies, nor am I in any way, fashion, or form attempting to speak on their behalf. What comes across in the following pages are my own thoughts and my own analysis of the situation in that country.

I am thankful, however, to the Ministry of Foreign Affairs and the wonderful staff who went out of their way to help me obtain interviews, writing letters in Russian (something I never could have accomplished), opening many doors, and cutting through red tape to speed up the process. I particularly want to thank Roman Vassilenko, someone who became a good friend, and all of his team for their support of this project and for all the help he offered, never tiring in answering my many questions, and forever correcting my Russian.

A book is never the work of a single person. I have many people to thank. First and foremost is my wife of nearly thirty years, Cynthia Nuckolls, who never tired of reading and rereading chapter after chapter, again and again, as the book slowly began to take shape. She offered suggestions and caught my mistakes, all the while providing invaluable research by digging through the Internet and my vast collection of books on Islam in search of just the right word.

I want to thank my good friends in Kazakhstan, Alibek Kimanov and his wife, Lyazzat Kimanova, for their help and friendship during my stay in their country. My translators, without whom I could not have done the work that I did—Lyazzat, Iliana Logutova, and Aizhan Bekkhozhina—not only translated but served as instructors of Kazakh life and culture.

Finally, let me add that any mistakes that may have made it past Hilary Claggett and the great team of editors at Potomac Books are entirely my own. And thank you, Hilary, for believing in the project from the very start.

ONE

Islam Without a Veil

"People underestimate their capacity for change. There is never a right time to do a difficult thing. A leader's job is to help people have vision of their potential."

—*John Porter*

A t the height of the Cold War in June 1963, the world stood precariously divided into opposing camps, with the Communist bloc on one side and the free world on the other. In what was to become a memorable speech, U.S. president John F. Kennedy stood in front of the Berlin Wall and addressed the world on both sides of the Iron Curtain: "There are some who say that communism is the wave of the future. Let them come to Berlin. And there are some who say in Europe and elsewhere we can work with the communists. Let them come to Berlin."

The future, as it turned out, did not belong to Communism, and twenty-four years after President Kennedy's speech another American president, Ronald Reagan, during what was to become another landmark speech, stood practically in the same spot by the Brandenburg Gate near the Berlin Wall. Addressing Soviet leader Mikhail Gorbachev directly, using his impeccable oratory talents acquired as an actor in Hollywood, Reagan challenged Gorbachev: "General-Secretary Gorbachev, if you seek peace, if you seek prosperity for the Soviet Union and Eastern Europe, if you seek liberalization, come here to this gate. Mr. Gorbachev, open this gate. Mr. Gorbachev, tear down this wall."

The gate was eventually opened and the Wall did come down, torn down not by Mr. Gorbachev but by thousands of people who were quite simply exasperated by the existing social and economic climate permeating the Soviet system. Of course the major political changes initiated by Mr. Gorbachev— his policies of glasnost, that of openness and transparency in government, and of perestroika, that of introducing major reforms in the Soviet political and economic system—helped pave the way for what was inevitable.

That, along with advancement in communication technology, made it no longer possible for the Soviet authorities to maintain their citizens in total political seclusion as they had in the past. Television and radio broadcasts from the West that in previous years had been jammed began playing a big part in sending the message to the people of the Eastern Bloc that there was a better life to be had through the democratic form of government.

Two other important developments contributed in bringing about an end to Communism in the Soviet Union. One was the arms race with the West, a race that was bankrupting the Soviets, who could hardly keep up with the United States and Western Europe, spending billions of dollars a year on arms, particularly when it came to developing weapons in outer space. The Strategic Defense Initiative (SDI) or, as it became known popularly, Star Wars, was President Reagan's initiative to partially force the Soviets to spend money they didn't have.

It was estimated that SDI cost the United States something in the vicinity of $100 million in research, and that it would be at least another ten years before it could reach the testing stage. It was enough, however, to frighten the Soviets even more, who saw in Reagan a staunch anti-Communist conservative, and who they believed would not hesitate to take the arms race to new levels.

And if that was not enough to load down the already crumbling Soviet economy, a devious plot by the Central Intelligence Agency to sabotage the Soviet oil pipelines was the West's coup de grâce.

___

At about the same time that the threat of Communism dissipated when the Soviet Union imploded, a new world order began to emerge. Perhaps it would be somewhat more appropriate to label the political climate that followed the meltdown of the Soviet Union as a new world *disorder*, in view of the turmoil and mayhem that was to come.

Despite the severe tension that prevailed between the East and the West in the Cold War years, precarious and unfortunate as they were for the millions living on the other side of the Iron Curtain under Soviet domination and the dictatorship of totalitarian rule, there existed a certain balance of power nevertheless.

That all changed with the demise of the Union of Soviet Socialist Republics (USSR) that left the political playing field to a single superpower and in the process created an imbalance of power. The end of Soviet rule over the Communist world brought about a tectonic change within the geographic area once occupied by the Soviet system. In turn, that change allowed new countries and new forces to emerge, among them Kazakhstan, which, despite a difficult beginning, has turned into a model for the rest of Central Asia to look up to.

There were both positive and negative outcomes of the unfolding events. On the positive side it gave the peoples of those countries that were until then part of the USSR the chance to govern themselves and to take control of their own destinies. On the other hand, the birth of new forces laid the groundwork for future conflicts. Indeed, the course of history changed suddenly in 1991 for millions of people when the Soviet Union ceased to exist.

In one of modern history's most fascinating moments, nations that were formerly under Soviet control found their freedom and independence almost overnight. Millions of people around the world watched in utter disbelief as crowds spontaneously assaulted the Berlin Wall—the very symbol of this East-West divide and where, in the past, East German border guards shot and killed people attempting to escape to the West. The crowds climbed up onto the infamous structure and began chiseling at it and eventually brought it down, stone by stone.

The collapse of the Berlin Wall was only the beginning. In the hours, days, and weeks that were to follow the rest of the Soviet empire began to crumble much as the symbolic wall. Some countries found the transition to democracy smooth, and other nations faced a harder time and only obtained their independence through strife and bloodshed.

Among those newly independent countries were the five former Soviet republics of Central Asia. These were countries that had largely remained in the shadow of Soviet Russia, countries of which very little was known and from which even less was heard in the West. When independence came these countries were ill prepared for the sudden thrust from Moscow's diktat to self-governance.

The new countries had to cope with the heavy responsibility that accompanies independence and the slow road to democracy that most had committed themselves to follow, of course with a gentle nudge from the West, mainly the United States and the European Union. The transition was not always an easy one, particularly when these countries had no prior experience in ruling themselves as modern states in the recent past.

Furthermore, most of the existing leadership had risen to power through the ranks of the Communist Party. This was the case with Kazakhstan and the rest of the former Soviet Central Asian republics. They had to learn about democracy and governance on the job, as it were.

The men and women who found themselves at the helm of their country when the Soviet empire collapsed had to learn how to govern peoples who throughout their long history had never been truly independent before, at least not in modern times. For the most part, many of the fifteen nations[1] that emerged upon the breakup of the Soviet Union had transitioned from one occupier or colonizer to the next.

At the same time this untested situation offered these emerging nations the chance to try something new, something different, perhaps a new experiment in nation building where mistakes of the past could be avoided. It did not turn out this way. Of the five former Soviet republics only one—Kazakhstan—succeeded in giving its citizens economic and political stability, as well as religious plurality. I will elaborate on that later.

The disappearance of Communism failed to bring peace and stability and the expected new world order. If new nations arose as a result of the Soviet Union's breakup, so did new political trends. At about the same time that the Berlin Wall came crashing down a new threat began to emerge as a new global conflict took shape, replacing the Cold War as the eye of the storm in world politics.

Before long militant Islam—also called Islamism—took over center stage and filled the social and political void left by the disappearance of Soviet Communism. Islamism became the new menace to world peace and stability and began to represent a clear and present danger to the national security of many nations, both Muslim and non-Muslim, democratic and authoritarian. Some scholars began to project this new conflict as one between the Muslim world and the West; others did not hesitate to call this conflict a clash of civilizations between Islam and the non-Muslim world.

There is, however, a certain analogy to be drawn between Communism in the 1940s and through the 1990s and the *Salafis* or *Takfiris* today, both in terms of real threat to global stability and in the manner in which the two systems function. As a system, Communism was an experiment in government that encapsulated far more than just running politics.

To some extent Communism dictated practically all social, economic, and political aspects of everyday life to those under its authority, except for dress and sexual behavior. Militant Islam, Islamism, *Salafism, Takfirism*, or whatever you would like to call it, as a political system, covers the same areas that Communism did, but then takes them a step further. Islamism dictates the way one should dress, the manner in which one should engage in sex; and the extremists go as far as banning music, songs, and dance. Neither Communism nor Islamism accept the existence of rival political entities within their system, each declaring themselves supreme, be it the Supreme Soviet or the Supreme Leader.

The Soviets thought they would resolve the issue of religion in the same manner that they tried to solve many other problems: by simply declaring the problem does not exist. They attempted to eradicate religion altogether and declared that there was no God. If there was no God, there was no need for religion.

The Islamists on the other hand are somewhat more pragmatic. They approached the problem from an entirely different angle: They incorporated God into their politics, insinuating that everything and anything they say or do is so directed by God Himself. They do not shy away from saying that they speak for God and in His name. Under Communism there was no place for religion in politics, whereas the Islamists have simply turned God into their politics.

The rules imposed by Communist regimes were strict and rigid. The death penalty, particularly in the earlier days of the revolution, was probably the most liberally distributed official document. In Islamist countries the death penalty is also easily handed out.

There was a tendency among some Communist revolutionary groups to believe that before the people would swing en masse into their camp and come out in support of the Socialist revolution, the domestic socioeconomic situation had to deteriorate and worsen considerably. The rationale was that if things reached a boiling point the people would rise up and side with the revolution. Their calculations were only half right. The people did end up rising in protest, but it turned out the protests were against the revolution.

Now compare the Communist modus operandi to that of the *Takfiris*. Ideology aside, it is practically identical. The *Takfiris* are banking on situations deteriorating to the point that the people will look to them for an answer. What other interest would they have in planting bomb after bomb in crowded markets, in mosques, and in crowded streets? Their regard for human life stands at about the same level that Communists held it. When the Islamic revolution in Iran overthrew the shah in 1979, the ayatollahs went about hanging hundreds of people from lampposts and construction cranes. Soviet dictator Josef Stalin would write in the margins of death warrants he would sign, condemning thousands of people to die the following morning, that "the numbers were too few."

Such is the degree of discontent with the political system in several Arab and Muslim countries that if free and fair elections were to be held today, it was long believed the winners would be the Muslim Brotherhood and its Islamist allies. However, the recent uprisings in Tunisia and Egypt as well as in Libya shed new light on that theory, one that Arab leaders helped propagate. The long-term implication of such an outcome would be disastrous for efforts undertaken by moderate countries such as Kazakhstan that remain committed to democracy and to a cordial entente between the East and the West. The weak point in any democratic form of government is that the benefits it accords its citizens—the right to vote and elect their representatives—can be used against it. Be it under Communist rule or that of radical Islamism, the outcome of such an election would inevitably be the same: one man, one vote, one time.

Another analogy one can draw between Communism and radical Islam is that just as Communism could not withstand the test of time and the natural will of its people to be free, neither will radical Islam succeed in the long run. The future belongs to the logical moderates who share a vision of peace and prosperity, who believe in pluralism and aspire to share the world's resources with others no matter what name they give their God.

In short, I believe the Islamist threat will eventually disappear, just as Communism disappeared from the Soviet Union. Socially and economically, the sort of environment offered by the religious extremists may look appealing to some youths who are fed up with the rampant corruption that permeates much of the Muslim world today. Many would like to have a say in how their countries are managed, and for lack of better choice will gravitate toward radical Islam, which promises a package deal: a better political and economic future on earth and a place in the afterlife.

But it is inevitable that, like Communism, radical Islam cannot survive in today's fast-paced environment of instant communication and globalization. Naturally, that does not mean the democracies should simply lean back and wait patiently for the system to implode. Rather, just as the West contributed to expedite the demise of the Soviet Union, so too it must happen in regard to radical Islam. Instead of an arms race, in this case the weapon of choice should be education.

Soviet-styled Communism and radicalized Islam are both philosophies that have been hijacked by extremists. While Communists and Islamist extremists live on opposing ends of the political spectrum, despite their great theological and philosophical differences, the two have much in common. It is therefore not inconceivable to imagine that someone like Osama bin Laden might have adopted Marxism had he lived in an earlier era.

In the final analysis, the Communism that was put into practice in the Soviet system was far removed from what Communism was initially intended to be, just as the version of Islam professed by the radicals is far removed from the true face of Islam, as practiced by millions of people around the world. In the end, some groups will have to adapt or simply disappear. Certain legitimate movements that have true representation in their national parliaments, such as Hezbollah in Lebanon or Hamas in the Palestinian territories, can adapt and join their country's mainstream politics.

Years ago when I first interviewed an official from Hamas, the Islamic Palestinian Resistance Movement, I was quite surprised by a statement he made. The interview got off to a bad start when about three minutes into the official's monologue, a monotonous diatribe that was undoubtedly a prepared speech he had delivered multiple times in the past, I realized I was just going to get the typical party propaganda line. I reached over and turned off my tape recorder, closed my notebook, pocketed my pen, folded my arms, and stared at him.

Looking somewhat surprised, the Hamas official stopped to ask what was wrong. I replied, very politely, that he must have been mistaken in thinking that I was an American tourist, or perhaps a newcomer to the region and its complex problems. I reminded him that I had been covering the crisis in the Middle East for the good part of thirty years. I told him that I had heard all the rhetoric before, which was all right for the general public consumption, but that unless he had something of interest to say, he was simply wasting his time and mine.

He looked at me with an intense glare for several seconds, though at the time it seemed much longer. I was starting to wonder if he was contemplating having his bodyguard shoot me. He then broke out into a smile and told me to turn on my tape recorder.

"We are well aware that the Palestinian people are not religious," he told me. "We recognize the fact that we are not about to change that anytime soon. We do represent a constituency and therefore we want to make sure that our rights are respected. The most we can hope for is to become like the Jewish religious parties in Israel, that is to say that we have our representatives in the government—two or three ministers in the cabinet—to ensure our voice is heard."

Just as President Reagan addressed Mr. Gorbachev, imploring him to open the Brandenburg Gate, a move that would facilitate dialogue and understanding between the East and West Blocs, reduce the political tension that prevailed at the time, and pave the path toward greater moderation, I cannot help but see a similarity in a growing trend among moderate Muslims and supporters of mainstream Islam asking that the "Gate of *Ijtihad*" be opened. We will look at the question of *Ijtihad* in greater detail in the following chapters and examine what it encompasses, and what it means to reopen those gates.[2]

─────

Since September 11, 2001, the Muslim world has come under attack in the Western media, some of it particularly brutal, especially the campaign spearheaded by the more conservative press. Granted, the attacks directed at the Muslim fanatics were deserved; however, blaming all Muslims for the attacks carried out by Muslim terrorists in New York, Washington, London, Madrid, Mumbai, and a host of other cities was ludicrous. Often the victims were Muslims, though that hardly registered in the West where mistrust of Islam grew to frightening levels.

Had the 9/11 attacks been carried out by nineteen Scandinavians, one can safely assume that the focus of the public and the media would have been to fear tall, blond men with pale complexions. As it turned out, the hijackers were all Muslim Arabs and the reaction was predictable.

One of the challenges facing the Muslim world is finding those who will speak for it. There is no central authority representing Islam as a whole. Generally one expects Saudi Arabia to be the accepted mouthpiece for Islam in view that the two holy cities, Mecca and Medina, are in Saudi Arabia and that the king carries the title "Custodian of the Two Holy Mosques."

But Saudi Arabia kept silent for the longest time after the attacks. Not only were the terrorists Muslim but fifteen of the nineteen were Saudi citizens, as is the mastermind of the attacks, Osama bin Laden. And yet the kingdom remained silent. There should have been an immediate response from the Saudis and a massive public relations campaign to put things in perspective. It's not as though the kingdom doesn't have the resources or the manpower; they retain some of the best and brightest people in the PR industry. But they chose to remain silent and there was no one else to speak on their behalf.

The Muslim world is far from being one. It is as diverse as the English-speaking world, where besides the obvious English-speaking countries—Great Britain, the United States, and Canada—one should include English-speaking countries in Africa (Cameroon, Nigeria, South Africa) and in other parts of the world like India, Australia, and New Zealand. The language as well as the accent differs greatly. The same can be said of Islam and how it is practiced in different parts of the world.

The form of Islam practiced in Morocco is quite different from that which is practiced in Saudi Arabia, and the Islam of Iran differs greatly from its closest ally in the Arab world, Syria, which is more of a secular state. Then there is the Islam one finds in a country such as Kazakhstan, where the approach to religion is drastically different than what one will find in Egypt or even in next-door Uzbekistan, Turkmenistan, or Kyrgyzstan.

Kazakhstan has adopted a very different approach to religion, where religion is simply not an issue as it often is in many other Muslim countries. Islam in Kazakhstan is moderate, separated from politics, and at peace with itself and with all other faiths and cultures. Kazakhstan is Muslim much as France is Catholic.

Islam in Kazakhstan gives us a very different picture than the one that has been popping up on the Six O'Clock News for the last ten years, where we have seen conflict and bloodshed and hate. A visit to Kazakhstan should be compulsory for any Western pundits who wish to call themselves "experts on Islam." A quick trip to Astana before hitting the airwaves on some of the conservative talk shows would go a long way in helping interfaith relations.

What they will find is a very different approach to Islam, and they may also learn that the war being waged by certain groups within Islam is not representative of the majority of the world's 1.6 billion Muslims. The extremists, also called Islamists, or sometimes wrongly called fundamentalists,[3] do not speak for all Muslims. It is therefore erroneous on our part, the part of the Western media, to label all Muslims with the same cachet as those who carry out terrorist attacks in the name of a religion that, at the base, is a religion of peace.

One of the problems facing the Western media in the aftermath of the 9/11 attacks was the fact that very few "experts" really knew the Muslim world. Even I, someone who has traveled extensively for long periods to twenty-four Muslim countries, was rather surprised when I visited Kazakhstan for the first time. Pleasantly surprised, I may add, to learn that there can be a very different form of Islam from the one we know in the Arab world.

As one American—a convert to Islam—I met at one of the interfaith conferences I attended in Astana stated: "The Islam practiced in the Arab world is not representative of all of Islam." Indeed, it is not. But as no one speaks for Islam in an official capacity, there is no unified, studied, and well-thought-out manner with which to respond to false accusations when they are directed at all Muslims. Often when a reply does come it tends to come from the mouth of some radical imam who spits venom and hate and lays all the blame on "the Jews and the Crusaders."

At the same time there is no central authority to speak *to* Islam in an official capacity and to hammer in the fact that violence is not the way of God. Whenever an attack occurred against any target, be it in the West or in the

Arab world, had there been a central figure to condemn those acts, things might have been different.

One of the more democratic aspects of Islam is precisely the fact that no one has the supreme authority to speak on its behalf or to address its followers with authority; however, that means that every Muslim can continue to speak not only for himself, but also can purport to speak for God.

For many Westerners who feel that Islam is in conflict with them, for those who fear Islam—those affected by Islamophobia—and believe that the Muslim world is on a jihad or holy war against the West, allow me to paraphrase President Kennedy when he made that historic speech near the Brandenburg Gate at the height of the Cold War. Allow me to say to those of you who believe that there cannot be a gentler, kinder, and more pragmatic face of Islam, let them come to Kazakhstan. To those who believe that all Muslims are a threat, let them come to Kazakhstan.

TWO

Islamophobia

"And if thy Lord had willed, He verily would have made mankind one nation, yet they will not cease to dispute." *Holy Quran (11:118)*

After the 9/11 attacks, with little or no regard for what mainstream Muslims said or did around the world and their attempts to differentiate themselves from the radical elements, in the United States many began to opine that there could be no understanding between Islam and the rest of the world. Some advocated that the gap was so distinct, so clear-cut, that there could never be any common ground between the House of Islam and the non-Muslim world whatsoever, based on the premise that Islam was out to convert the world or kill those who resisted conversion.

Legions of "specialists" descended unto television and radio talk shows armed with quotes from the Quran (translated into English), justifying—at least in their own minds—their fears of Islam. Those who understood what Islam stands for and saw no threat from Islam as a religion in turn used the same Quran to explain that the opposition's interpretation is not at all what was meant. Of course nothing is ever clearly defined in either politics or religion—now combine the two and you end up with a truly explosive cocktail.

At about this time, that is to say not long after the terrorist attacks on the World Trade Center and the Pentagon, a new disease appeared on the world's political scene. It was called "Islamophobia," or the fear of Islam. What exactly is Islamophobia? To better understand what it means we need to dissect the word. The word "phobia" is defined in the *New Oxford American Dictionary* as "an exaggerated, usually inexplicable and illogical fear of a particular class of objects or situation." Note the definition includes the word, "inexplicable." In other words, a phobia is an irrational fear, one that cannot really or logically be explained but is still feared.

Islamophobia is a hatred or fear of Islam or Muslims, especially when feared as a political force. Yet many of those who fear Islam don't exactly know why they fear it. The fear is inexplicable and illogical, based on ignorance, lack of any real understanding of Islam, and often accompanied by a rejection to learn anything about the topic in question from objective sources.

Some self-proclaimed experts by Islam regurgitated pure nonsensical rhetoric, as this item published by an American Internet news source demonstrates: "It is time we admitted that we are not at war with 'terrorism.' We are at war with Islam. . . . The idea that Islam is a peaceful religion hijacked by extremists is a dangerous fantasy."[1]

———

Shortly after the 9/11 attacks, while tempers were still high and some Americans continued to pour French wines and champagne down the gutters because France, as well as many other countries around the world, voiced its opposition to a U.S. plan to attack Iraq, one of my neighbors in suburban Virginia sported a bumper sticker on his car that read "Nuke 'Em!" I asked him whom he wanted nuked, who was (th)em? His reply was somewhat vague. "The terrorists," he said. Fine, I would like them nuked too; the trouble is that they are among a civilian population. Should we nuke innocent women and children in the process?

Indeed, many of the symptoms of Islamophobia arose mainly from lack of knowledge of the religion and what it stands for. The majority of those who responded to the self-call to arms against what they perceived to be invading hordes of *Takfiris* who would rampage through the streets of middle America, sword in hand, ready to decapitate anyone refusing to prostrate themselves five time a day while facing Mecca, had rarely—if ever—been to a Muslim country. Among those who professed that all Muslims were part of some sort of secret cabal plotting to undermine the democratic system of government in the free world were a number of respected scholars. Again, many had never set foot in a Muslim country.

Yet because the nineteen terrorists who attacked America on September 11, 2001, were Muslims, many people in the United States saw this as an attack by Islam. They tended to forget that among the three thousand killed in the World Trade Center towers were also many Muslims. This is not to mention the fact that Sunni Muslims are not organized into a monolithic group but that every imam has equal authority. There is no equivalent to pope, cardinal, archbishop, or bishop in Sunni Islam. There are imams and every country has a grand imam. But auto-defenses went up instantly and every Muslim became a potential terrorist in the eyes of many Americans. And the most frightening thing was that this line of thinking was found at all levels of society, including among the highly educated.

––––––––

For the record, I do not claim to be a scholar, although I have lectured as a guest speaker at more than a dozen of the top universities in North America, and I did teach public diplomacy for a few semesters at my alma mater. I was published in scores of international newspapers and respected journals and appear on more than forty radio and television channels as a commentator on Middle Eastern affairs, including the BBC, VOA, CNN, FOX NEWS, Radio France International, and others.

As a journalist I have covered the Middle East and its associated problems for the good part of thirty years, based in the region more than half that time. With the exception of Libya and Sudan, I have visited and reported from every country in the Middle East multiple times, with extended stints in Lebanon, Egypt, Syria, Jordan, the Palestinian Territories, the United Arab Emirates, Kuwait, Iraq, Iran, and Turkey.

My formative years were spent in Lebanon where I grew up, raised as a Catholic, but living in what was in later years described as "Muslim West Beirut." Because of this, I can claim to know Muslims fairly well—good and bad ones.

I grew up with Muslims. I went to school with Muslims—to Catholic school, I may add. I socialized with Muslims. During my teen years, when I stopped going to church on Sunday, my best friend at the time, a Sunni Muslim, and my Lebanese Jewish girlfriend would each grab me by an arm and force me into church to please my mother. They would remain with me throughout the service, standing and sitting along with the rest of the congregation. During my junior high school days, when economic times were tough and the Christian grocer down the road refused my mother credit, it was the Muslim restaurant owner and the Druze greengrocer next door who gave us credit.

This is not an attempt to apologize for the bad things happening in the world being committed by bad Muslims. Placing all Muslims in the same basket with the fanatics who have given a great religion a bad name is shortsighted, plain wrong, and does a disservice to all mankind. Exacerbating the situation is the fact that it wasn't just the non-Muslim world that contributed to the rise of Islamophobia.

This ignorance of the true face of Islam was present on all sides. Muslims who misquoted the Hadith—the sayings of the Prophet—and the words of the Holy Quran to fit their political ambitions made this new ailment worse.

In fact the vast majority of Muslims are God-fearing and decent people, trying hard to make ends meet, like most everyone else today. As Javed Mohammed, the former president of the Islamic Society of North America, stated, "There are between five and eight million Muslims in the United States and twelve to fifteen million in Western Europe. The vast majority of Muslims are not anti-American or anti-democracy or anti-freedom."[2]

Regrettably, those are facts that Americans often tend to forget. "It will require a conscientious effort to fight the negative stereotypes that equate Islam with fundamentalism, terrorism, subjugation of women, and the other misperceptions."[3]

As a rule, says Radwan Masmoudi, president of the Washington-based Center for the Study of Islam and Democracy, Muslims do not disagree that the Quran is the word of God. What Muslims continue to argue over and constantly disagree about are the meanings of certain verses and how they can apply to different situations. When taken out of context, most of the verses of the Quran could be misunderstood or misapplied.

Alas, this is something that is all too common and allows anyone with an agenda to interpret the verses as one sees fit. The writings of the Quran are so complex, and they are written in such a flowery manner, that any one sentence can easily be explained in more than one way. Masmoudi explains in a special report produced by the United States Institute of Peace[4] that a science known as *asbab an-nouzoul*, or the reasons or causes for the revelation, was developed in order to understand the specific reason, such as the conditions at the time, that would relate to any particular verse.

Indeed, ever since the horrific terrorist attacks of September 11, 2001, by nineteen Muslim terrorists, Islam has come under the spotlight time and again. "Islam, it seemed, was under siege," wrote Professor Akbar S. Ahmed,[5] the Ibn Khaldun Chair of Islamic Studies at American University in Washington, D.C.

To be sure, what emerged in the aftermath of 9/11 was not a pretty picture, as militant Islam went on a spree of violence. Hijackings, bombings of public transportation systems, televised beheadings of innocent hostages. The terrorists did not make any distinction between men, women, and children, nor between combatants and civilians. They slaughtered not only "infidels," but many Muslims too. Many were attacked as they prayed in mosques or were on pilgrimage to Mecca, Medina, Karbala, and other holy cities. Bombs were detonated in crowded market streets in Baghdad or Kabul where mostly women shopped. The attacks were widespread and there seemed to be no logic to them, other than to inflict the maximum amount of casualties and damage. In the end, they most probably have killed more Muslims than non-Muslims.

As for the attacks on the World Trade Center and the Pentagon, all it took was nineteen men to stain the name of one of the world's three great religions and to open a schism between the mostly Judeo-Christian West and the mostly Muslim East.

This violence committed in the name of Islam by the fanatics did not represent the true face of Islam to the majority of believers (*al-mu'qmeneen*), nor to the knowledgeable Western scholars and analysts. These argued at times, against the mainstream current often portrayed by the popular media, that this was not the true face of Islam. Islam had been hijacked. The images of Muslims who sought to kill and maim that were flashed across television screens around the world were those of a fanatic minority, a small, albeit dangerous, percentage of the world's 1.6 billion Muslims.

———

As has been proven time and again, creating havoc does not require numbers, just a few diehards convinced of their cause and willing to fight and die for it, in one fashion or another. As an example, at the height of the "troubles" in Northern Ireland, when the Irish Republican Army terrorized and para-lyzed London, planting bombs around the British capital, all it took was about 150 men and women to keep the British army in a state of constant alert and deployed throughout the British Isles. In fact the real hardliners, the crazies that went about planting bombs and assassinating people, were most probably no more than a few dozen.

Though few in number, these nineteen fanatics who participated in the 9/11 terrorist attacks were strong enough to make themselves heard around the world, and they were bold enough to bully the millions of mainstream Muslims into remaining silent, for the most part.

As John L. Esposito, professor of religion at Washington's Georgetown University and a respected authority on Islam, pointed out, "Governments, policymakers, and experts around the globe debated whether political Islam or 'Islamic fundamentalism' is a multifaceted and diverse phenomenon or a uni-formly clear and present danger to be consistently and persistently repressed and eradicated."[6]

Islam, it seemed, was on a collision course with the rest of the world's religions. "With Judaism in the Middle East, Christianity in the Balkans, Chechnya, Nigeria, Sudan and sporadically in the Philippines and Indonesia; Hinduism in South Asia and after the Taliban blew up the statues in Bamiyan, Buddhism," according to Ahmed.[7]

Ahmed goes on to say "that with the scholars driven out, or under pres-sure to remain silent, it is not surprising that the Muslim world's educational achievements are among the lowest in the world."[8] This lack of education is one of the main, if not the principal, engines driving the current conflict within Islam and between Islam and the rest of the world.

This, and the lack of tolerance, is driving the fanatics and giving them a solid base. What is needed, therefore, to combat this predicament is precisely . . . education and tolerance. Indeed, we are likely to hear much more about education and tolerance in the coming years, especially if a number of pro-posals put forward in June 2010 by Kazakhstan at a meeting of the OSCE in Astana are acted upon.

"Tolerance," said President Nursultan Nazarbayev of Kazakhstan in his keynote speech delivered at the opening session of a two-day conference on tolerance and interreligious understanding in Astana, "is one of the most important issues in Europe post World War II." Nazarbayev called for the creation of an OSCE center for nondiscrimination and tolerance and for the appointment of a high commissioner for interethnic and interreligious tolerance. Addressing delegates from the fifty-six member countries of the OSCE, Nazarbayev said that his country has always been "a cradle of tolerance and understanding, focusing on inter-confessional harmony."

The Kazakh president warned, however, that religion can divide rather than unite people, unless inroads are made to educate the people to accept each other and to respect their differences. Now, many will argue that the last thing the world needs is yet another UN- or EU-type entity with scores of highly paid bureaucrats producing reports that no one will ever read. But this is one idea worth acting upon because of its simplicity and because it tackles the very basics of the problems facing the world today.

Tolerance will come about through education. People will stop looking at others as potential threats to their ethnic group if they learn to understand that the "other" has the same wants, fears, and needs that they do. "There is a need to unlearn the fear of the other and to unlearn xenophobia," said Jorge Sampaio, the European Union's representative speaking at an OSCE meeting in Astana in 2010 that was aimed at addressing the issues of integration. "People are not naturally hot-wired for intolerance. They are taught to hate." And just as they are taught to hate, they can "unlearn" to hate. Of course this is a long-term process, but it is also the only way the world will solve its problems of racial, religious, and ethnic intolerance. The media also plays a big role in this project, as it can help promote understanding or it can help promote strife. "With patience and strong public diplomacy we can gain hearts and minds," said Sampaio.

Those hearts and minds can be won through a well-studied public diplomacy campaign to educate the people and to prove that myths about the "other" are simply that: myths. But there are two major stumbling blocks for the organizers of this campaign. How do you prevent the messages of hate and warmongering from being sent out, all while maintaining freedom of expression and speech? The answer is, of course, education, education, and more education.

This is precisely the line being followed by Kazakhstan. So, what is it that makes Kazakhstan stand out among other countries with Muslim majorities as an example in tolerance and interethnic understanding? Multiple factors have affected the Kazakh approach to interethnic cohabitation and collaborative coexistence. Some can be credited to the country's historic tradition of hospitality. It is partially the Kazakh tradition to show respect for all peoples of all faiths and nationalities that has influenced this country's pragmatic approach, but much of the credit goes to the strong belief by the country's leadership in, and their efforts to promote, intercultural and interfaith dialogue that has helped turn this policy into a success.

According to Javed Mohammed, "Muslims for their part need to look and reflect on the events of the past century and understand how we got into this state, and how to get out without playing the blame game."[9] But if Islam seemed heading for a clash with other religions, those who know Islam well know that the real vision of Islam offers a very different picture, indeed.

While the conflict pitting Islam against the West was widespread as the result of the work of these fanatics, it was not universal. That was the redeeming factor in this conflict and proof that Islam was not the enemy and should not be seen as the enemy. There were many Muslims who did not agree with the narrow views of the fanatics.

There are "pockets of resistance," one may say, and they play an important role in helping avoid an open confrontation with the West. There are a few Muslim countries where this appealing trend of "liberal Islam" exists and offers hope that there can be a meeting of the minds between Islam and the West, or rather between Islam and modernity. Such is the case in Kazakhstan, where a more moderate form of Islam exists, and Muslims (the majority) live at peace with a wide range of religious groups, including Christians, Jews, Hindus, and Buddhists.

We should make a point of studying the Kazakh model and examine its inner workings. What we will find is a very different form of Islam—one that other Muslim countries might want to consider using as their model. The main challenge, however, is getting the countries in question to accept the fact that change is needed. And even then it would still be difficult for the moderates to convince the hardliners that change would benefit all.

THREE

Kazakhstan Emerges

"Religion is no longer an 'opiate' numbing the people into docility; it is more like speed."

—*Akbar S. Ahmed*

With Kazakhstan assuming the chairmanship of the Organization for Security and Cooperation in Europe it will be in a position to influence the politics in the region." Those were the words of Zbigniew Brzezinski, one of the most knowledgeable Americans when it comes to matters having to do with Central Asian politics.

Brzezinski is the former national security advisor to President Jimmy Carter, who spoke to me from his office at the Center for Strategic and International Studies in Washington when I directed a quick question his way while I was with the *Washington Times* in Astana. Brzezinski was quick to recognize the important role that Kazakhstan can play in helping contain the volatile political situation in Central Asia, with a war in Afghanistan now ten years in the making and with no end in sight.

Add to the above continuous political rumblings in several of Kazakhstan's neighboring countries, including a violent change of regime in Kyrgyzstan in 2010, the third in recent years. And not too far away, the Pandora's Box of Central Asia, a nuclear-armed Pakistan sitting precariously on the fence, rocking dangerously between the pro-democracy, U.S.-backed alliance and the pro-Islamist, pro-Taliban, and pro-al-Qaida elements, many of whom are in positions of power in the country's military. Should Pakistan fall under the influence of the latter, it would give the Islamists access to nuclear weapons, a move that would greatly alter the geopolitical map of the region.

Brzezinski added: "Furthermore, Kazakhstan has itself a stake in the region and in the filament in Afghanistan and Pakistan not spreading." Few, but very accurate words.

––––––––––

As one of the pillars of stability in Central Asia, Kazakhstan is directly concerned in making sure that the region remains calm, or in any case as calm as possible. Kazakhstan has a vested interest in what transpires across its borders, as it could very easily become affected.

Political instability is highly contagious, which is a good reason to try to maintain and contain the political, social, and economic environment, not only in one's own country, but as the world becomes more connected, it pays dividends to make sure that our neighbors also get a piece of the pie.

It's been two decades since Kazakhstan became independent and this could be as good a time as any to examine its achievements.

Accusations of human rights abuse aside, this country has been the most successful of the former Soviet Socialist republics of Central Asia. Regrettably, the issue of human rights will continue to surface so long as there remains an ounce of accusation or suspicion that this sort of activity is continuing. Having said that, the initial report card looks encouraging enough. From all angles of the social, economic, and political spectrum this country has fared rather well. From a political perspective Kazakhstan has remained stable, an achievement not all countries in the region can claim.

The country is doing far better than most of its neighbors when it comes to keeping the unemployment rate down and the economy moving forward. Kazakhstan continues to attract workers from other countries, whereas practically no Kazakhs went to work as laborers in the other former Soviet states of Central Asia.

While in a meeting with some scholars from the Kazakhstan Institute for Strategic Studies, I asked a question about Kazakh migrant workers going to work in the neighboring countries of Kyrgyzstan, Uzbekistan, and Turkmenistan, wanting to know if there were any figures available. My translator did not even bother translating the question; instead she just answered the question herself: "No, there are none." I asked her to translate nevertheless. The reply from the scholars was identical. "No, there are none."

But in the other direction, Dr. Anatoly G. Kosichenko, head of the Kazakhstan Department of Culture and Religion Philosophies at the Institute of Philosophy and Politology, said there are a million immigrants from Kyrgyzstan, of which 15 to 20 percent settled in Kazakhstan, while the rest migrated on to Russia.

And finally, from a religious angle, Kazakhstan emerged head and shoulders above the rest of the region, if not of the world, when it comes to religious understanding, integration, and lack of prejudice. Kazakhstan, no doubt, has demonstrated to itself first, to the Muslim world second, and finally to the world community at large, that Islam does not have to be on a collision course with other religions in order to survive and thrive. Islam does not have to stand alone and outside the mainstream to succeed as the world's fastest-growing religion.

Kazakhstan has demonstrated that one can follow Islam and at the same time remain fully open and receptive to outside ideas and not feel threatened by them. In fact one of the most intriguing aspects of the Kazakhstan experiment in government and religion is in its striving to achieve understanding among different communities, religions, ethnicities, and nationalities. Perhaps the fact that the country counts between 120 and 140 different religious and ethnic groups had something to do with the Kazakh outlook on the world and on religion.

Kazakhstan has proven that a mostly Muslim nation does not have to be at odds—nor at war—with the rest of the world. Kazakhstan has demonstrated that Islam can be just as any other religion, at peace with itself and at peace with the world. As it turns out, this Central Asian republic has worked fervently to bridge the ugly schism that has developed between Islam and the West since the 9/11 attacks and subsequent invasions of Arab and Muslim lands by American armed forces and their allies, actions that at times were described by some Muslims as a "crusade" against Islam.

Kazakhstan, under the leadership of President Nursultan Nazarbayev, has succeeded in navigating out of Soviet totalitarianism, sailed across the sea of turbulence that surrounded the country, and maintained a steady course despite much criticism from the West for a poor human rights track record. Civil wars, coups, and counter-coups became all too common in the region, except in Kazakhstan.

The country remained on a steady course heading toward democratizing its political system and its society, despite the lack of any real historic foundation of a democratic past, as for example was the case with other parts of the Soviet Union and its satellite states.

Kazakhstan and the other republics of Central Asia had to learn about democratization and self-governance on the job, so to speak. Nation building takes time, but the Khazakhs never had the luxury of time to build up institutions and practice proper governance prior to independence. They never had the time to transition from one system to the other. Rather, they had to take the plunge practically overnight from a Soviet-controlled Socialist state into a free-market economy. They were expected to adopt and adapt to Western-styled democracy instantly. Otherwise, they came under heavy criticism.

Never mind the fact that it took the United States close to two hundred years to get where it is today in terms of democracy. And despite the fact that the United States sees itself as the guardian of world democracy, it, too, committed human rights abuses in the treatment of suspected Islamist terrorists arrested, captured, or traded for financial reward.

The leaked images of Iraqi prisoners being tortured at the Abu Ghraib detention facility in Baghdad are but one example. Another stain on Western democracy is the treatment of prisoners at Guantánamo Bay, Cuba, where a judicial limbo was intentionally created by the U.S. government in order to deny the prisoners their constitutional rights. Had the prisoners been incarcerated in detention facilities on the U.S. mainland, the government would have been obligated to grant them certain privileges as called for by the constitution and by U.S. federal and state laws.

Never mind that it took the Europeans several centuries to reach the political maturity Europe enjoys today. Never mind that it took them countless wars—including two world wars in the twentieth century that have devastated the continent, destroyed entire cities and towns, killed millions of people and displaced tens of millions more, creating the largest wave of refugees the world had ever witnessed. As we have learned from George W. Bush's largely unsuccessful experiments in nation building in Iraq and Afghanistan, imposing Jeffersonian democracy upon countries that have never experienced it does not guarantee it will work.

Democracy is a very complex and intricate system of governance that requires some fine-tuning and decades of political maturity, if not longer. There cannot be a one-size-fits-all, off-the-shelf democracy that the West can export to nations with different cultures and different social structures and expect to work in a similar manner to established Western democracies.

To believe that such a feat is doable, to believe that what took more than a century for Europe and the United States to achieve is possible right away, is to demonstrate a sense of political immaturity and to show complete ignorance as to the importance of local traditions in a modern political system. As Winston Churchill used to say, democracy is the worst sort of government except for all the others that have been tried.

In the course of attempting to implement social changes in a country, one must consider local elements and local customs as well as the socioeconomic fiber and structure of the nation. Some societies must take into consideration certain elements, such as the all-important role played by the clan, the tribe, the family, religion, and the weight these carry with different family members. While some of these fabrics of society are largely alien to Westerners, they play a central role in many if not most countries in the developing world. In order to ensure that transition from past to present systems of governance is successful in the long run, some countries are obliged to take these elements into account or else risk failure.

Kazakhstan is one of those countries. Kazakhstan's president has come under repeated criticism for failing to implement ample democratic reforms. However, what the critics of the Kazakh government failed to realize is that implementing a democratic form of government in different societies necessitates different approaches. It would be ludicrous to expect residents of Central Asia, who have no recollection of self-governance or of a democratic past, to react the way that Estonians, Lithuanians, Latvians, Poles, or Bulgarians reacted when the Berlin Wall came tumbling down.

Western diplomats based in Astana, the newly founded capital of Kazakhstan, are among the first to agree that while still short of the goal of attaining democracy as perceived by Western standards, Kazakhstan is well ahead of the other four former Soviet Socialist republics of Central Asia—Kyrgyzstan, Tajikistan, Turkmenistan, and Uzbekistan. There is no question as to the amount of progress this country has achieved in just twenty years of independence.

In an exclusive interview President Nazarbayev granted me for the *Washington Times* in April 2010, just before he headed to Washington to attend a nuclear summit, the Kazakh president said: "We can argue for ages with our critics about whether or not Kazakhstan fully meets the standards of democracy in their Western understanding. One can also argue about whether it is fair at all to separate standards of democracy into Western and Eastern understanding." Fair? Well, maybe not. Pragmatic? Certainly more so. Democracy, much as any form of government, needs to be shaped and molded to fit the country one is applying it to.

Nazarbayev said that the East does not agree with the stance that the Western way of life and views should be "the ultimate truth." Perhaps that is one of the shortcomings of Western nations, expecting the entire world to adapt to their line of thinking, regardless of times, locations, and pricing structure.

"The world is diverse," said the Kazakh president. He went on to explain that Kazakhstan is a nation in transition that is following a new way of building democratic institutions "on the basis of and in accordance with our reality and traditions." The president stated that over the years of independence Kazakhstan has consistently moved along the course of democratic reforms based on its own national interests.

As Bruno Antonio Pasquino, Italy's ambassador to Kazakhstan, and several of his Western colleagues have stated, democratic reforms have been and are being conducted in Kazakhstan regardless of whether there is or isn't any criticism. Those reforms, said the president, were based "on our interests, realities, and current regional situation. It is important to note that our society did not have the experience of democratic development, like the one that was accumulated, for example, by Central and Eastern European countries. Democracy is a long-term process that acquires new facets and shades in the course of time. Kazakhstan is in the early stages of this way."

Responding to his critics, President Nazarbayev fired back:

Basic human rights are ensured in our country—these are the right to a decent life, education, health care, freedom of religion, right to learn one's native culture and communicate in one's native language.

What is most important is that equal rights are ensured for representatives of all 140 ethnic groups and 46 religious denominations and that trust and stability are maintained. At the same time, we have proceeded from the principle "economy first, politics second." And throughout all the years of independence we have consistently moved along the way of advanced economic development and increasing living standards, consecutively supported and followed by political liberalization.

————

From the OSCE to the Organization of the Islamic Conference (OIC), Kazakhstan has stepped up to the plate as it assumed the chairmanship of both prestigious organizations just a year apart.

The country is playing a major role in world governance, guiding international bodies through a crucial time in geopolitics when the Judeo-Christian world found itself on the brink of a clash of civilizations with Islam, as some scholars have insinuated.

What the world is going through today is not so much a clash of civilizations as it is an identity crisis within Islam itself. The world's fastest-growing religion is facing serious strife from within and, as a direct result of this internal struggle, Islam has opened itself to attack from without. While the actions of certain countries and organizations may have been seen as contributing to the escalation of the crisis between Islam and the West, Kazakhstan labored hard to better these relations.

When I received the following e-mail from a reader last summer, I thought the questions raised in the e-mail were the sort that Kazakhs would raise at one of the many conferences organized by the Kazakh government as it tries to promote peace and understanding among the different religious groups.

"Many Muslims around the Islamic communities in the West are suffering as a direct result of the radical elements within Islam that have hijacked our religion and turned it into a faith of terror. These radical elements make us look like barbaric, uneducated, uncivilized people."[1] The reader went on to say, "Non-Muslim friends in the West have every right to be critical of Islam and question the Quran. Why are we still silent, while they totally shame our faith? Why do we blame the West, America, or any one else . . . ?" The problem, said the reader, is "within Islam." He continued: "It disgusts me that our Islamic leaders can not or will not recognize this problem and deal with it." The reader then asked a few basic questions, not really expecting anyone to provide answers.

Why there is so much hatred towards Islam?

Why is the Islamic community allowing terrorists to hijack their religion to justify their hideous evil attacks on Western countries?

What are the true "moderate Muslims" doing to prevent this abuse of our religion by their radical brothers and sisters in Islam?

Isn't it the responsibility of every moderate Muslim to claim ownership of Islam, and openly denounce any Muslim using the Quran to justify their evil acts?

Do you agree that when the civilized Islamic community takes control of Islam, people might view us in a different light and we might regain our dignity?

There are good odds these questions will surface at some point during Kazakhstan's tenure at the head of the OIC. But there are also a number of other questions that arise. For instance, why was Kazakhstan able to maintain its Muslim heritage and remain on track toward modernization, while a few other Muslim countries imposed strict sharia (Islamic) laws upon their citizens, clamped down on individual freedoms, and persecuted all who would not adhere to the diktat of the ruling theocracy?

Why is Kazakhstan's society so outgoing and so free-spirited, while other Muslim countries force women to wear the chador or burka, the head-to-toe black garment, or the abaya, the black wrap women are obliged to don every time they wish to leave their homes?

What makes Kazakhstan stand out among other countries with Muslim majorities as an example in tolerance and interethnic understanding? According to the country's president, there are four reasons. One: The age-old tradition of the Kazakh people of showing tolerance and respect to other peoples and their ethnicities. Two: Making tolerance a key point of the country's policy. Three: Avoiding double standards. Four: Being an active supporter of dialogue and working to promote dialogue between the Muslim world and the West. An official government publication distributed by the presidency states that Kazakhstan has had no religious or ethnic conflicts on its territory since independence twenty years ago. The publication goes on to state that religion was suppressed for so many years that it became immaterial, and that it continues to occupy little of everyday life.

These and many others are just some of the questions regarding the Kazakh phenomenon—the success story of Central Asia—that this book will attempt to address. While some of its neighbors have been bogged down in economic woes, civil strife, and wars, in just twenty years—one generation— since independence Kazakhstan projected a very different image of what people traditionally think of when they think of a Muslim nation.

While there is no doubt as to the Muslim identity of the country, where the typical greeting in Kazakh is the traditional Muslim salutation *as-salamu aleykum* (peace be upon you), Kazakhstan is proof that there can be a gentler, kinder face of Islam, where the religion can live at peace with itself and with its neighbors, despite their differences. Kazakhstan can be the model for the rest of the Muslim world on the path to moderation.

FOUR

The New End Game in Central Asia

"The enemy is not Islam, the great world faith, but a perversion of Islam."

—*John Cornyn, U.S. senator (R-TX)*

As a relatively new nation, Kazakhstan is somewhat of a paradox. Kazakhstan is barely twenty years old, yet at the same time it is a place with a rich history going back centuries in time, to the days when Genghis Khan and the Mongol warriors roamed the steppes of Asia on horseback, and even earlier. In fact, according to some historic records, it was the Kazakhs who domesticated the horse, or at least the people who lived in the region that is modern-day Kazakhstan.

Nomadic tribes have been living in the region since the first century BC, though some historic records indicate that the region has been inhabited at least as far back as the Stone Age. History often provides the key to better understanding a nation and its people. If you want to get a better grasp of where a country is likely to go in the future, study its past. Anyone involved in the study of current affairs will attest that current affairs are not entirely current. Much of the work involves delving into the past as we try to predict the future.

In ancient times nomadic nations ruled the land that is roughly the territory of modern-day Kazakhstan between the fourth century and through the early thirteenth century, at about the time of the Mongolian invasion. A number of administrative districts were established under the Mongols in the territory, which eventually became the Kazakh Khanate.

Two of Kazakhstan's major cities, Taraz and Turkestan, were founded along the northern route of the Great Silk Road around medieval times. The modern Kazakhs emerged from a mixture of tribes living in the region around the fifteenth century, and they had developed a common language and culture by the sixteenth century.

Today Kazakhstan is a (mostly) Muslim country with a laid-back and open-minded attitude toward religion, and it is a land where all religions are treated equally. Call it Kazakh tradition, perhaps, but there is a certain attitude toward life where all beliefs are granted equal respect. This is not something you find in abundance in this part of the world—Kazakhstan is an exception.

The people of Kazakhstan are free to make up their minds whether they want to worship God or not, and if they choose to do so, they are equally free to choose which god they elect to pray to. Muslims, Christian Orthodox, Catholics, Protestants, Buddhists, and Jews, as well as dozens of other sects and religions, are free to worship and congregate at will and without risk of reprimand, worry of arrest, or having to constantly look over their shoulders for fear of being beaten and/or arrested by government thugs, by an overzealous religious police force, or by some vigilante group.

In that sense, Kazakhstan is almost unique in the Muslim world. The only other Muslim country that may compare with Kazakhstan in that regard is Lebanon, another country with an important Christian population—but the pre–civil war Lebanon, not the morass it has turned into since.

Another paradox is that Kazakhstan is a country in Central Asia that often likes to think of itself as being more European at heart than Asian, despite the fact that it is geographically at the very center of Asia and shares a long border with China. Europe, meanwhile, is some six to seven hundred miles away from its western border. Almaty, the country's principal city and former capital, is less than an hour's drive from the Chinese border. Still, one cannot help but feel the attraction that Europe has for Kazakhstan, as Italy's ambassador Pasquino said, a sentiment echoed by his French colleague, Ambassador Jean-Charles Berthonnet. This is a mutual feeling because Europeans, too, want very much to maintain the European character of Eurasia, as stated Ambassador Pierre Morel, the European Union special representative to Central Asia.[1]

"We have had a growing interest in Central Asia in the last years," said Mr. Morel. "The East-West line is very important. We want to keep the European character of Eurasia. These countries have been related to some dimension to the European civilization through the Soviet education system."

And an even greater paradox is that all while feeling European, Kazakhs do not feel any less Muslim. The wonderful vision of Islam that Kazakhstan projects is in the openness with which its people approach religion. Call it modern Islam, if you like. For example, it is not out of the norm in Kazakhstan for young Muslim women to wear a small Quran on a thin gold chain around their neck, as many Muslim women around the world tend to do. The major difference in Kazakhstan is that these women will wear the Quran while dressed in a rather revealing manner and dancing the night away in one of Astana's clubs where alcohol is abundant. And no one here blinks an eye. This would be unimaginable in some other Muslim nations. Granted, this is only a snapshot of one aspect of life in Kazakhstan and of course it does not represent any deep theological views. It's a tiny detail, but life is made up of tiny details.

Religion in general and Islam in particular is looked at through a very different lens in Kazakhstan than the way Islam is perceived in more conservative societies in the Muslim world. While this sort of dress code may be frowned upon in some countries, to a less conservative individual it underlines the fact that Islam can be adaptable to all lifestyles. You don't necessarily have to wear a veil to be a good Muslim.

"Many Muslims believe that they must choose between Islam and modernity or Islam and democracy," says Masmoudi.[2] This is a false choice, adds the president of the Center for the Study of Islam and Democracy. "When faced with this decision most Muslims would choose Islam and reject anything that they regarded as alien or contrary to the principles of the faith."

Kazakhstan is also a paradox because officially the country qualifies as a democratic country, enough in any case to be granted the rotating chair of the OSCE, the very international body tasked with ensuring that free and fair elections are held regularly in emerging democracies. Yet the government of President Nursultan Nazarbayev often stands accused of dragging its feet when it comes to implementing democratic reforms in its own country. The legitimacy and fairness of elections in Kazakhstan are at times questioned by international observers, as well as by human rights groups. Outside Kazakhstan, many people have a false impression about the country, its politics, and its human rights record. While not denying that those abuses did take place, it is also necessary to point out that there is still a certain element of democracy in Kazakhstan that is unfounded in the rest of the region. Even the opposition is cognizant of that fact.

A few years ago I was invited to participate on a media panel in Almaty, Kazakhstan's principal city. Minutes after checking into my hotel I received an invitation from a member of the political opposition to attend a press conference. The e-mail said to meet in the lobby and that the organizers would provide transportation. I joined a group of fellow journalists in the lobby, where a gaggle of plain-clothed policemen were trying—unsuccessfully—to blend in.

Moments later, two minivans pulled up outside the hotel and ferried us off to the event. The first speaker delivered his opening address, stipulating that Kazakhstan was a police state and that the government was committing crimes and that people opposed to the government were turning up dead, or simply vanished. I followed up with a question, asking that if indeed this was a police state, how did he explain the fact that the secret police who were with us since we left the hotel made no attempts to prevent us from attending the event. Nor did they take any steps to discourage the opposition members from holding their press conference, as would have very likely happened in many police states.

"My dear sir," shot back the member of the opposition. "This is Kazakhstan, this is not Uzbekistan or Turkmenistan."

The truth is that the Silk Road to democracy is not always smooth. True, much has been said and written about governments of countries in the developing world that have at times failed to respect the democratic principles they initially set out to respect and implement—and rightfully so. Voices should rise up in defense of democracy, free speech, and the right to a free press. Reporting such travesties of injustice is the duty of a free media. But sadly, far less is said or written when those same countries take steps in the right direction, building on the foundations of still young and inexperienced emerging democracies.

In most countries where the media is controlled by the government, individuals are afraid to speak their minds openly. A sure sign of an improving situation is when people begin to speak up, no longer looking over their shoulders, even if all is not yet quite as smooth as it should be.

"We don't have an ideal situation regarding the media in Kazakhstan," Mirbulat Kunbayev, the president of the newspaper editors club in the Kazakh capital, a group made up of about one hundred editors representing progovernment media, told me recently.

Kazakhstan qualifies as a democratic country, though the former Communist republic has been governed by the same man since the country obtained independence twenty years ago. Nazarbayev initially came to power in 1989 as the head of the Kazakh Communist Party and was eventually elected president of independent Kazakhstan in 1991.

Opposition groups in the country have accused the president of appointing close relatives to top government positions, although that practice is not seen through the same lens as it is in most Western countries because of the importance family ties occupy in society.

One question that often pops up from Western visitors to Kazakhstan is, what happens to the homeless people when the temperature plunges to around −35 or −40 centigrade, as it often does in winter? The answer is quite simple: there are no homeless people among the Kazakhs.

Everyone belongs to a clan, a tribe, and a family. Family members who are better off will try to help relatives in need, and if the immediate family cannot help, then help is sought higher up the chain. That system has been in place for centuries, and in spite of rapidly changing social trends and the displacement from the steppes to the cities of what used to be a largely nomadic society, it continues to work.

The "system" will look after its members and no one ends up living on the street. Family values and traditions are deep-rooted in Kazakh culture. Alibek, one young Kazakh instructor I met, was able to name his grandfathers on his father's side going back sixteen generations. Erlan Karin, a high-ranking official in the ruling Nur Otan Party, can name twelve of his patriarchal ancestors. "Any Kazakh should be able to name at least seven of his ancestors," Karin told me when I interviewed him in his Astana office.

Kazakhs are comfortable with their past and seem to enjoy a special relationship with their history. Unlike their two giant neighbors, China and Russia, modern Kazakhstan does not have to compete with the role that the older Kazakhstan played in history, as do the great powers.

Perhaps one may find an explanation here somewhere as to why Kazakhs are without complex when it comes to religion. In order to better understand where Kazakhstan stands today, it is important to understand also how it relates to and with Moscow—its former master—and to compare that with its developing relationship with Washington—its (hopefully) future best friend. Additionally, one must not forget that militant Islam is now a contender in the new great game.

Both China and Russia, who once commanded great empires throughout Central Asia, are today competing with their former selves, trying to prove that they remain a super regional power. Astana does not have the chip on its shoulder that Beijing and Moscow seem to carry. The people of Kazakhstan know where they came from, and they are proud of their heritage. In that respect they do not have an identity crisis. The pertinent question for Kazakhstan is more along the lines of where they are going. The country seems to be an island of prosperity caught in a sea of destitution. A simple look at a map is enough to explain somewhat where Kazakhstan is today, and not just from a geographic point of view.

When you are not a major power, for a regular country like Kazakhstan, the pressures that come simply by bordering major powers must be tremendous. For Kazakhstan the pressure could not be stronger—Russia to the north, China to the southeast. While Kazakhstan has no direct border with Mongolia, there are only about one hundred miles or so separating the two countries, a distance that over the centuries never seemed to deter the Mongols from invading. In the west Kazakhstan shares a water border with Iran across the Caspian Sea, and to the south it borders two former Soviet republics, Uzbekistan and Kyrgyzstan.

As they say, you don't choose your neighbors. A former Lebanese ambassador in Washington used do complain that "we live in a bad neighborhood." And he was not referring to the embassy or the residence, both situated in one of D.C.'s nicer neighborhoods.

The political pressure from Russia and China must be immense, but problems arising from some of the more unstable former Soviet republics are of a very different sort, the latter occasionally going through revolutions and counterrevolutions, periodically sending droves of refugees in search of a safer political and/or economic environment to Kazakhstan's borders.

These refugees add to the country's financial burden and rightfully justify the government's nightmare worries of economic troubles. Furthermore, Kazakhstan is worried by the problems of migration posed by some of these refugees, some of whom may be connected to *Salafi* groups and who may come to Kazakhstan with the intent of recruiting young followers. Although the *Salafis* adhere to nonviolence, unlike their bretheren in the *Takfiri* groups, nevertheless *Salafis* and democracy hardly go hand in hand. A quick peek at a map showing where *Salafis* are in the majority and control the government, and the country as a whole, is enough to convince anyone still debating the issue. Additionally, political migrants from neighboring Uzbekistan are promoting militant Islam in Kazakhstan, said Bulat Sultanov, the director of the Kazakhstan Institute for Strategic Studies, at a conference in Astana in July 2010.

If modern-day Kazakhstan is at ease with its past, it faces somewhat of a challenge when it comes to establishing its national identity and solidifying it for its future. Indeed, establishing a strong national identity is a crucial prerequisite needed to ensure the survival and continuation of the modern nation that is Kazakhstan today. And if the Kazakh notion of openness and tolerance of others is to be encouraged, then it is of great importance to the region and the rest of the world for Kazakhstan and the Kazakh approach to politics and religion to survive and to encourage other countries, other sects, and other groups to adopt this notion of multiethnic and multireligious harmony.

What makes Kazakhstan stand out is that, unlike many of the recently emerged democracies or countries on their way to becoming democracies, where typically the country is composed of a single ethnicity, or perhaps, in some cases, the population is made up of two prominent ethnic and/or religious groups, Kazakhstan has to juggle with the sensitivities of some 140 different faiths, ethnic backgrounds, and cultures.

In addition to the complicated mosaic of faiths and cultures, today Kazakhstan is also trying to establish its rightful place between its geographic location in Central Asia and its geopolitical position, that of somewhere between post-Soviet Asia, Europe, and America. One of the unique political characteristics of Kazakhstan is its ability to maintain a successful bipolar foreign policy that has placated both East and West, allowing Astana to enjoy cordial relationships with both Moscow and Washington.

———

What contributes to this unique approach to geopolitics? An approach we also find reflected in the manner in which the country manages its relationship with regard to religion. Perhaps it has to do with its geographic position? The manner in which the country successfully juggles its foreign policy and its internal diversity is no easy feat, particularly in a part of the world that is at times prone to violence.

Of course the Cold War is over and the Kazakhs are now masters of their own destiny, and that plays a big role in how Astana handles its international relations. The fact that today Russia and the United States have a common enemy has somewhat helped pave the way for Kazakhstan to get closer to the United States without raising too many red flags in Moscow.

The irony in this post–Cold War world is that Russia and the United States now find themselves fighting the same enemy—radical Islam—an enemy that Washington had helped establish, train, finance, and equip in Afghanistan after the Soviets invaded in 1979.

The rise of fundamentalist Islam represents a clear and present danger, not only for the United States and Russia but for all of the world's democracies, as well as for any society that believes in pluralism. Today the former U.S. ally is fighting the presence of American troops in the country with the same vigor it fought the Soviets. For any society that believes in pluralism in this world, the soft and discreet shout from the heart of Kazakhstan, calling for more understanding among different peoples and different religions, must not fall on deaf ears.

———

If al-Qaida, one of the main Islamist groups currently on the U.S. terror list, has kept the U.S. military and intelligence communities occupied for the past ten years, so too have other groups of Islamists in Chechnya and Dagestan kept the Russians on the alert. The immediate danger to the free world today is what to do if any of those groups manages to acquire weapons of mass destruction.

The belief at the time was that godless Communism could be fought by God-fearing religious groups. No thought was given to the risks involved in starting something that could—and did—spiral out of control. Today both Russia and the United States are focusing on combating this new world threat.

This is yet another reason why Kazakhstan has a vested interest in giving Islam a gentler and kinder face. The idea is to promote the values and assets of moderate thinking and to keep the fundamentalists and fanatics at bay.

No doubt it is the Kazakh temperament that may have something to do with the country's soft approach to Islam—that and the fact that the nation had to learn to live next door to China and Russia and retain its vast territory. That philosophy seemed to have worked over the decades and no doubt contributed to giving the Kazakhs that unique sense of survival that the country and its people still retain.

Take for example Kazakhstan's relationship with Russia. Amazingly, Kazakhs bear no grudges against the Russians, despite the fact that the country was occupied for nearly sixty years by the Soviets, who were often not too kind toward the Kazakhs, and not to mention centuries of tsarist domination prior to the Communist revolution. Kazakhstan's history with Russia had been tumultuous and some times were tougher than others. In the final days of tsarist rule there were a number of uprisings against Moscow, the most serious of which occurred in 1916. The Kazakhs' biggest complaint, though, was the systematic destruction of their nomadic way of life.

Kazakhstan's maintaining of cordial relations with Moscow does not prevent it from being the most pro-American country I have come across in travels that have spanned eighty-three countries, with perhaps the exception of Israel, but that's a different story altogether.

Although many people in Kazakhstan still speak only Russian, they make an effort to communicate their appreciation when they meet an American, and the Kazakh government appears to care far more for exposure in the American press, more precisely in the Washington press, than in any other country, including Russia. What does that tell us? It tells us that the government in Astana wants the powers-that-be in Washington to know what it is doing. It tells us that Astana cares more about what Washington thinks of its foreign policy than it cares about what Moscow thinks of its foreign policy. Kazakhstan's leadership is well aware that its future as well as its security, while closely tied to Russia's foreign policies, lies in being even closer to those of the United States.

The United States was the first country to recognize Kazakhstan on Christmas Day in 1991. The first U.S. embassy was opened in Almaty the following

January, and the embassy subsequently moved to Astana in 2006 after the capital was officially transferred in 1997. Before independence the Soviets had integrated Kazakhstan into the USSR, but growing tensions inside the Soviet Union led to a demand for vast reforms, both in the political and economic fields.

Still, there are no lingering ill effects and Kazakhs continue to extend their hospitality to Russians, as well as to any other traveler to this almost mystical land. Russians are not despised the way they are in Afghanistan, for example. Relations between the two countries are excellent and the foreign ministers and presidents of the two countries exchange visits practically on a monthly basis. There is no visible animosity toward the former occupiers. Quite to the contrary the people of Kazakhstan, for the most part, still look to Russia for part of their cultural heritage. Russian is spoken at all levels of society, although not very successful efforts are afoot to promote the Kazakh language, part of the Turkic family of languages.

The Russian language remains predominant with the majority of the country's newspapers, and many Kazakh intellectuals continue to consider that Moscow universities still offer the best higher education in the world, though no Russian institution of higher learning appears on the list of the world's top one hundred universities.

The special relationship that the Kazakhs and Russians enjoy proved to be an asset when Kazakh foreign minister Kanat Saudabayev embarked on a preliminary fact-finding/peace-building visit to the Caucasus after Georgia and Russia went to war over the breakaway autonomous regions of Abkhazia and South Ossetia.

Upon receiving the nomination of the OSCE chair, Kazakhstan wasted no time investigating ways in which to bring about fruitful and peaceful solutions to the various lingering conflicts that were troubling the region. "The Kazakhstan chairmanship is much more resilient in the face of Russia's position," Grigol Vashadze, Georgia's foreign minister told me in early 2010, after a meeting with his Kazakh counterpart in Tblisi.

Soon after Kazakhstan was granted the OSCE chair in 2000 was when its foreign minister began his fact-finding mission to some of the troubled spots in the region. Kanat Saudabayev's efforts were praised by all sides as he conferred with other leaders over the Nagorno-Karabakh dispute between Christian Armenia and majority-Muslim Azerbaijan, and the Caucasus war between Georgia and Russia over Abkhazia.

Supporting the Kazakh foreign minister's efforts was Alcee L. Hastings, (D-FL), a member of the U.S. House of Representatives representing Florida's twenty-third congressional district and co-chair of the Helsinki Commission. During a meeting in Vienna at the OSCE headquarters the U.S. lawmaker told me: "If anyone can say 'no' to the Russians it is Kazakhstan."

Perhaps one thing that Kazakhstan shares with the United States is that the populations of both countries are made up of a multitude of minorities. The United States is often referred to as the melting pot where people from all countries, all races, and all religions of the world converge and learn how to get along, leaving their ethnic luggage at the borders. An interesting trait about immigrants to the United States is that even when two members of opposing sides in an ethnic conflict meet in an American city they seem to get along. Once they return to their home country, that's another matter altogether. The same can be said about Kazakhstan, to some degree. Kazakhstan welcomes people from all over Central Asia who at times are engaged in conflict, but once in Kazakhstan they, too, leave their ethnic, religious, and political luggage at the borders. Or in any case they hide it well enough so that it doesn't show.

For years while under Soviet rule, Kazakhstan was Moscow's favorite dumping ground for everything and everyone it considered undesirable. Under that heading came nuclear waste from the USSR, as well as millions of people who ended up on the wrong side of the Communist Party. Many found themselves in that category because they either disagreed with Moscow or were suspected of holding "counterrevolutionary thoughts" and would possibly eventually disagree with Moscow. But Stalin, for one, did not like to take chances, and as the dictator liked to say, "A million deaths is a statistic."

Some people were simply thrown off cattle trains as they pulled into stations, the train slowing down, but not even stopping. At times, tens of thousands of people were given less than an hour to pack a lifetime of belongings into a single suitcase before they were exiled to Kazakhstan. There were ethnic Germans, Ingushetians and Chechens, Georgians and other minorities from the

Caucasus, along with Lithuanians and Bulgarians and many other nationalities—anyone whom Moscow deemed to be an outcast or might have threatened the Revolution. Many of them died along the way, others arrived to face the harsh winters of the steppes where the temperature reaches forty degrees Celsius.

Most of these newcomers arrived with no food and little clothing. The newly arrived exiles were greeted with open arms by the people of Kazakhstan (the majority of whom are Muslim) who took these foreigners (mostly Christians) into their homes, which was often nothing more than a yurt, the large tent that is typical for this region. They were offered food and clothing and shelter. Today most, if not all, of these different nationalities and ethnicities have kept their languages and traditions alive, and today the challenge is how to keep all these different groups united as one nation.

When the Soviet Union collapsed and independence was granted or grabbed, "Kazakhstan was the only successor state whose titular group was an ethnic minority (39.7 percent)," wrote Edward Schatz in a 2000 article published in *Europe-Asia Studies* titled "The Politics of Multiple Identities: Lineage and Ethnicity in Kazakhstan."[3]

The Russians comprised 33 percent of the population, and years after Moscow pulled out many still remain. Germans and Ukrainians made up 4 percent each, with Belarusians, Uzbeks, and Crimea Tatars at about 2 percent each. Today, Kazakhs represent slightly more than 60 percent of the population.

The consequences of using Kazakhstan as a nuclear dumping site are still felt in the city of Semipalatinsk, where babies continue to be born with horrific deformities. Over the course of some forty years the Soviet Union conducted 465 nuclear explosions at the world's largest nuclear testing site. According to Saudabayev, "The cumulative power output of these explosions equated 2,500 Hiroshima-size bombs. More than 1.5 million people suffered from these tests in Kazakhstan and vast territories became absolutely useless for life."[4]

At independence Kazakhstan found itself to be the world's fourth largest nuclear power, having inherited its arsenal of weapons of mass destruction from the Soviet Union. As a mostly Muslim nation, Kazakhstan was approached by other Muslim countries with lucrative offers to attain those WMD. Officials in Astana would not reveal which countries had made the offer, but it's not very difficult to make an educated guess.

There are very few Muslim countries with enough money in the bank, scientists who have the knowledge of how to handle the nukes, and the need and the desire to have access to nuclear weapons. Saudi Arabia comes to mind, as does Iran. Kazakh officials would not elaborate on the issue. The world would have been a very different place today had the Kazakhs been tempted by the offer.

To quote Saudabayev again: "In the early days of independence there was no shortage of foreign emissaries asking our president to keep the nuclear weapons, saying that you are going to be the first and only Muslim nation with nuclear weapons and that you are going to be respected by the whole world."[5]

Just emerging from the Soviet sphere and with few assets in the nation's coffers, the offers of financial compensation were indeed tempting. But Kazakhstan resisted and chose to voluntarily give up its nukes, and under U.S. technical assistance the country's entire nuclear arsenal was eliminated, along with stockpiles of biological and chemical agents.

This was by no means free and came with a price tag of some $240 million covered by the United States. Still, it was a relatively small price to pay to get nuclear weapons out of circulation and to make sure they would not fall into the wrong hands at some later point. But if the battle to control the country's WMD is over, the fight between outside powers to maintain influence over the region continues.

This political tug-of-war has been going on for the good part of two hundred years. Rudyard Kipling, the great British poet and writer, described the political duel for control of Central Asia as the Great Game. Fast forward to 2010, and the Great Game is still being played out on much the same playing field, albeit with some adjustments. First, as Ambassador Pierre Morel, special European Union envoy to Central Asia, pointed out at a lecture in Washington in 2010, the Great Game is no longer being played by two nations. Now each of the countries concerned has their say, and a major difference this time around is the involvement of China. I would add another all-important player in this very serious game, and that is militant Islam.

Other changes that jump to mind is the fact that Great Britain is no longer the great power it once was and has ceded its place in the game of geopolitics to the United States, now looking out for Western interests, or rather looking out for U.S. interests, shall we say? Russia, who in the interim has lost two empires, the first under the tsars and the second under the red banner, is still struggling to remain in the new game.

For Russia this game carries great significance, as it is being played out in "the near beyond," as Moscow likes to refer to its former domains, now independent states. Naturally, whatever transpires carries a direct impact on the countries of Central Asia, and among them Kazakhstan.

But this time around the situation is somewhat different and far more volatile than it was two hundred years ago. First, there is far more serious competition from two newcomers, China and politicized Islam. The People's Republic of China is the up-and-coming power to be reckoned with from a political and economic perspective. Already the Chinese are buying more oil from Saudi Arabia than the United States. With its middle class growing in leaps and bounds and gaining greater purchase power, the Chinese are buying cars almost as fast as they can be imported. Wherever cars are concerned there is a question of oil, and when you say oil, you have to think in terms of geopolitics on a vast scale. What happens in one part of the world will automatically impact what is happening on the other side of the globe.

The other newcomer to this great geopolitical game, one that could greatly upset the Central Asian applecart if certain measures are not taken to prevent it, is political Islam, which carries influence not only in Central Asia, but in countries ranging from Russia's Pacific coast to the Caucasus. As the planet has truly become a global village, the dangers presented by Islamist extremists are equally as real in the United States as they are in Kazakhstan. Keep that in mind as we move forward and look at Russia's role in Central Asia, and more specifically in Kazakhstan.

Additionally there are now the voices of the independent republics of Central Asia that need to be heard. The colonial era, when two powers were able to call all the shots, is long resolved. Among these new voices is that of Kazakhstan, the new dynamic factor in Central Asia, and it is a voice that is becoming more active and that wants attention, as it represents the new direction and the new energy of the region.

The other new voice in Central Asia is Islam. Since the fall of Communism in 1991, Islam has resurged throughout Asia. After the defeat of the Soviets in Afghanistan the United States declared victory and lost interest in the region's severe social and economic problems. The army of U.S. advisors who had helped defeat the Soviets returned home, leaving the mujahideen, who had been a staunch ally, to fend for themselves. The Islamist movement grew rapidly under the radar, as not enough focus was given to this movement and it was allowed to prosper, consolidate, and grow and eventually take over Afghanistan.

Monday-morning quarterbacking is always an easy exercise, but chances are that had al-Qaida not attacked the United States on September 11, 2001, the United States would have never invaded Afghanistan, and chances are that the *Takfiri* movement could have expanded easily from Afghanistan into other neighboring states, moving under the radar, as it had in Afghanistan.

On the fifth commemoration of the 9/11 terrorist attacks on New York, the Pentagon, and Pennsylvania, President George W. Bush delivered a speech to the nation as he tried to explain what went wrong in Iraq and Afghanistan. By then the United States was involved in two full-fledged Middle East and Central Asian wars. Bush said that Osama bin Laden had a multiphase strategy that was to have been carried out in the months and years after September 11, the ultimate aim of which was to reestablish the Muslim caliphate.

Stage one was to expel the U.S. forces from Iraq. Stage two was to establish an Islamic authority, or emirate, which would be developed until it achieved the level of the caliphate. Stage three was to extend a jihad wave to the secular countries that border Israel. Stage four was to trigger a clash with Israel.

It took five years of war for the president to divulge this information to the nation. Only eight days after the attacks, on September 19, 2001, I had written an analysis of the war for United Press International titled "The Potentate of the Super-Stan," where I outlined what I believed was the plan of the *Salafis*, based on conversations I had with numerous sources in the diplomatic and intelligence worlds. Central Asia played a big role in the Islamist plan.

What transpired was that, much like any revolution, the Islamist movement needed to continue to grow or it would perish. In his quest for Muslim expansion, bin Laden would have liked to see the "Balkanization," or in this case the Islamization, of Central Asia. Upon reflection, Islamization is the wrong term because there is little that is Islamic about bin Laden's combat, other than name. "Bin Laden's ways are not Islamic at all," Professor Akbar Ahmed told me during a conversation we had in 2003.

Bin Laden turned to Islam as his vehicle to launch a war against the non-believers much like Pol Pot used Communism in Cambodia in the 1970s. Had bin Laden been politically active in the 1960s or 1970s, he could have as easily adopted Communism as a platform to propel his cause. But mix in religious fervor and any revolution becomes all the more potent, dangerous, and explosive.

While bin Laden and the Taliban were not talking openly about a greater Islamic entity, others, such as *Al-Muhajiroun*, a group based in Britain and with whom bin Laden enjoys close ties, were talking actively about a caliphate.

Bin Laden's first step was to hijack Islam to fit his cause, passing himself off as a fervent religious man. That, of course, is meant to win him the support of hordes of fanatics who know little, if anything, of the Quran. On the other hand, as the leader of al-Qaida, bin Laden knew exactly what he was doing and where he wanted to take his movement. Bin Laden's long-term project will be easier to comprehend if one is armed with a map of Central Asia.

Afghanistan, where bin Laden had set up camp, is a desolate country without much of an infrastructure, staggering under a heavy burden of lawlessness, economic troubles, unemployment, and the resurgence of the Taliban. Following the harsh years of Soviet invasion, war, and a disastrous civil conflict, all the ingredients of a failed state were present—in other words, a perfect place from which to launch a revolution.

Much of Afghanistan's terrain is inaccessible except by mule or horseback, making the task of modern armies impossible. With the exception of a handful of special forces units who receive additional special training, the modern military machines are dependent on motorized vehicles for transportation and logistics.

The Afghan warrior is used to his country's geography and to its rugged conditions—just ask the Russians. To the south and east of Afghanistan lies Pakistan, another country that sits on the fence of Muslim fundamentalism. The Taliban warned Pakistan that siding with the United States would bring down the wrath of the Muslim world upon it. Pakistan, an Islamic country, is in a most precarious situation.

The percentage of the population that supports the fundamentalists is in question, but some analysts believe the Taliban enjoys strong support in the army and the intelligence services. This gave the country's ruler at the time,

General Pervez Musharraf, a very fine line to tread. It also made him an important friend of the United States and the Western coalition. "The situation for Pakistan is very difficult," said Mr. Ahmed. "Pakistan is between a rock and a hard place. Musharraf is sitting on a tiger. You either ride it or you are inside its belly."

With its nuclear capabilities, Pakistan would represent an ideal asset for bin Laden and the Taliban, should it fall off the fence and into their hands. Think of the consequences. Regardless, bin Laden's next step would be to extend the reach of his Muslim fundamentalism. Tajikistan, to the northeast, Uzbekistan to the immediate north, and Turkmenistan to the northwest—all three are former Soviet republics with whom Afghanistan shares a border and a common religion. And Kazakhstan is the icing on the cake, a huge country with considerable oil reserves. Besides geographic expansion, which would make this caliphate one of the largest countries in the world, controlling all those countries would give them greater power in numbers (a combined population of more than 120 million), and these countries come with a wide range of natural resources, not least of which is oil.

Turkmenistan borders the Caspian Sea, a short hop to Azerbaijan, another former Soviet republic and a Muslim country. Given that scenario, the new Muslim caliphate governed by bin Laden or the Taliban, the next step would be to encircle Iran, itself a Muslim nation and rich in oil and other natural resources. Look at the map again and see the implications for the rest of the oil-rich Arabian Gulf. Iraq, Kuwait, Bahrain, the Emirates, Saudi Arabia, and Oman are only a small step and a revolution away.

Remember the old domino effect theory much feared by the West—especially the United States—during the Vietnam War? Now look at the map again: we are back in the Middle East. Palestine, Israel, Jordan, Egypt, North Africa, and sub-Saharan Africa are the natural extension for bin Laden's caliphate. Think this is an unbelievable scenario? Too farfetched? It was done a few centuries ago. Bin Laden is far too astute to content himself with living in the caves of Afghanistan. Read between the lines of his communiqués and the picture will become much clearer.

Addressing a meeting of some two hundred French ambassadors gathered at the Elysée Palace in August 2007 for the Fifteenth Ambassadors' Conference, French president Nicolas Sarkozy stressed the urgency of what he called "the first challenge" facing the West: How to prevent a confrontation with Islam.

"The threats we face today—terrorism, proliferation, crime—know no borders," warned Sarkozy. "There's no point in waffling: this confrontation is being called for by extremist groups such as al-Qaida that dream of establishing a caliphate from Indonesia to Nigeria, rejecting all openness, all modernity, every hint of diversity. If these forces were to achieve their sinister objective, it is certain that the twenty-first century would be even worse than the last one, itself marked by merciless confrontation between ideologies."

––––––––

Understand the above dilemma and you may start to understand why Kazakhstan is so concerned by issues of terrorism and religion, although it has not been directly affected by either of those two issues as much as other countries in the world.

When studying political developments in Central Asia it is important to look at Russia's foreign policy in general before turning to take a closer look at the manner in which it impacts its former domains, given Russia's continuing concerns, involvement, and interests in the region. It is equally important to take into context what is happening on Russia's other borders, too, as the outcome will influence decisions in Moscow and those will ultimately impact the countries of Central Asia, including Kazakhstan. That domino effect from the 1960s works just as well in Central Asia.

Russia continues to regard what happens in the "near beyond," a region that includes Kazakhstan, with great interest, but Russia's problems are threefold. On its western flank it is struggling to keep NATO as distant as possible from its borders, and not doing very well at it. Several former members of the now-defunct Warsaw Pact joined NATO shortly after the collapse of the Berlin Wall.

On its western flank it is trying to maintain some influence with its former Soviet republics and satellite states, and fighting to preserve its access to oil, and to keep its hand in the new battle emerging over oil pipelines and pipeline routes in territories that were once part of the vast Soviet Union. When the book is closed on Russia's monumental mistakes of all time, after selling Alaska to the United States because Russia thought it was a frozen wasteland with no value attached to it, loss of the "stans" must certainly come in a close second.

Oil pipelines are becoming as strategic today as oil itself was in the 1970s. Control the pipelines and it no longer becomes necessary to control the oil itself or the oil producing countries, a task that has always been fraught with pitfalls, as was proven in Iraq. The better solution is to train the oil producing countries to defend their own facilities and let them do the job.

Rather, today the power rests with those who control the pipelines and the land through which these pipelines cross. For the United States and Western Europe, new pipeline routes means not having to be 100 percent dependent on Russian and Ukrainian monopolies. For Russia, controlling the pipelines means retaining power in the "near beyond."

The United States, while preoccupied by the war in Afghanistan, is most likely to push ahead with plans to secure the terrain to build pipelines through the war-torn country, especially if oil is discovered in large quantities, as is expected. Another former Soviet republic, Azerbaijan, rich in oil, needs a secure route for it, other than the existing ones through Russia.

One option is to pipe it through Afghanistan and south into Pakistan and to ports where supertankers can take it to markets in the West, as well as to the new growing market in the east. Energy—oil and gas—from the Caspian Sea basin are at the center of what is truly happening in Central Asia today.

Why the sudden importance of this new route? Nearly 40 percent of Europe's gas comes from Russia via pipelines that run across Ukraine. New routes are desperately needed in order for the West not to remain dependent on a single route or on a single supplier. For the longest time, all oil from Central Asia flowed westward through Russia and Ukraine.

Now enters the dragon, China, with a rapidly growing middle class that is able to afford new cars, and a demand for oil consumption that is growing exponentially. Expected capacity of the new China pipeline is going to be around 700,000 barrels per day initially, and that is expected to be doubled within the next four years to 1.4 million barrels per day.

Slowly but steadily China is emerging as a nation that can no longer be ignored in Central Asia. This again is an area where the players are impacted and where Kazakhstan's role, given its geographic expanse, is an important one. Pipelines can now flow eastward from Kazakh fields, taking away the quasi-monopoly retained by Russia until now.

There is much truth to the old adage that history repeats itself. As a journalist and chronicler of history I have found it not unusual for the day's top stories to resemble pages right out of a history book. Journalists, after all, are the ones who write the first draft of history. As I mentioned in my previous book,[6] where mega-computers and black magic have failed to predict the future, history books have succeeded.

To some extent, and with a little bit of an analytical mind, one needs only to read up on the history of a region in order to be able to predict the future. Take Afghanistan for example, a land that many have conquered but never really ruled. From Alexander the Great to the British to the Soviets, and now the Americans, none have really been able to tame and subdue the Afghan warrior.

Between the early 1800s and the early 1900s Great Britain and the Russian Empire were engaged in a vicious political tug-of-war in Central Asia, one that at times turned violent. Both Russia and Great Britain wanted to control the all-important corridor leading up from the warm waters of the Gulf and north through Iraq, Iran, what is presently Pakistan, and Afghanistan.

Imperial Russia, much like the Soviet Union, needed an outlet to a warm-water port that could be used all year round, unlike the Baltic ports that freeze during the long harsh winters. This led to the great diplomatic rivalry and occasional clashes between the two superpowers of that time. Some of the battles were fought by proxy, with each side subcontracting their war or part of the war to third parties.

The now infamous Blackwater company, which hired tens of thousands of mercenaries to help U.S. forces in Iraq and Afghanistan, in fact presented nothing very revolutionary in terms of how wars are being fought. This sort of thing had been going on for centuries. Now fast forward to today and you will see that little has changed in that part of the world. Foreign powers are still fighting over the same land, and at times by proxy. Russia is still struggling for access to a warm-water port, as it was under the tsars. It was in fact this very need that led to the invasion of Afghanistan by the Soviets in 1979.

Today Russia, though no longer imperial and no longer Soviet, remains nevertheless worried that it could be denied that strategic access, crucial for its navy and its defenses. Moscow's major naval facility on the Black Sea in the Ukrainian port of Sevastopol in Crimea is currently being leased from Ukraine, a lease that expires in 2017. What happens then?

For the moment and so long as the current president remains in power in Ukraine, Moscow has little to fear. However, Russia cannot hope that the same Ukrainian government will forever remain in power. Ukraine is now a democratic country where elections are held at regular intervals and Moscow has no guarantee as to how long the government in Kiev will remain friendly toward the Kremlin. The previous government had already asked the Russians to pack up and go. But if the geopolitical situation is changing on Russia's western flank, in Central Asia very little has changed in the centuries-old fight for control of the land known today as Afghanistan, a vital link between routes crossing from west to east and north to south.

China, the new player in the east, whose influence is growing in leaps and bounds, worries both Moscow and Washington. Just how influential China is in Central Asia is obvious by the way Beijing has cornered the market in Kazakhstan, for example. Just about everything one finds in Kazakh stores, from computers and furniture to notebooks and electronics and imitation iPhones sold at about one-eighth the price of the genuine article, now comes with a "Made in China" label.

And here comes the big novelty in the Central Asian geopolitical game: oil. With China's economy growing at a healthy and steady pace, so too is its insatiable appetite for oil. For the first time oil from the Central Asian nation of Kazakhstan is going to be flowing east. Until now all the oil from Kazakh fields flowed west to Russia, Ukraine, and Europe. A new pipeline of some 1,384 miles is being constructed to carry the oil from Kazakhstan to China. This pipeline is owned jointly by the China National Petroleum Corporation (CNPC) and the Kazakh oil company KazMunayGas, and it runs from Kazakhstan's Caspian shore to Xinjiang province in China.

"This is Kazakhstan's most important oil export pipeline now and in the future," Julia Nanay, an analyst with the Washington-based PFC Energy, a company specializing in global energy strategy, told the *Washington Times* in early 2010. Indeed, since the discovery of vast oil and gas reserves in Kazakhstan, the country has been able to invest considerably in developing its infrastructure, consolidating its economy, and investing in its future by subsidizing the education of its youth in an innovative way.

As one can see, things are moving at a steady pace in Central Asia, where the Great Game has in fact become even greater, although this is hardly the same game with the same rules as when Kipling wrote his book.

With the threat of Islamists now added to the playing field, the stakes have become greater. This last point is what makes Kazakhstan's position as an honest broker between the East and West all the more relevant. Kazakhstan can use its position in politics, commerce, and trade to help shape better relations between the East and West.

In politics it used its influence as a major mover and shaker in Central Asia to help shape the region; in commerce and trade it used its natural resources to build a modern nation; and in religion it fell back on its understanding of how societies should get along with mutual respect for each other. Some call it "the 'Kazakhi' way."

FIVE

The "Kazakhi" Way: Economy First, Politics Second

"If they analyze the situation as thoroughly as they should, Muslims will realize they are the first targets. What are the fundamentalists really after? Simply taking over Islam and then turning its back on modernity."

—*Alexander Haig, former U.S. Secretary of Defense*

During my six-month assignment in Astana, the capital of Kazakhstan, I was often struck, as any foreigner in a foreign land will be, by some of the unusual behaviors that one typically notices in a new environment but that is unnoticed by longtime residents until someone mentions it. I am talking about small things, everyday things, things that have to do with daily life or the workplace. Often, people never pay much attention to these "anomalies" because they grew up around them.

For example, when I lived in Belgium I had a hard time adapting to the traffic rules that allowed cars to your right to shoot out into oncoming traffic, giving them the right of way, even though you were driving on a major thoroughfare. You can thank Napoleon for that one.

Having lived in Cairo as a child, it never occurred to me just how unsanitary was the way laundry was pressed in Egypt when you sent your clothes out to be cleaned. The *maquagi*, or the person who does the ironing, would take a large sip of water from a glass or container kept nearby and then spray the clean clothes with their mouth to dampen them. It's a brilliant idea and ingenious for a country where resources are scarce and one needs to be inventive. Except, in this case, the clothes are dampened *and* covered with the *maquagi*'s germs. It wasn't until my wife remarked how unhealthy it was that I really noticed.

Cairo taxi drivers will honk their horns every few seconds, even when they are driving on a straight road at 3 a.m. and without another car or pedestrian in sight. Residents of Tripoli in north Lebanon will eat a local type of meat pizza, *lahmajeen,* placed inside a large pita bread. That's the equivalent of eating a pizza sandwich. The list, I am sure, can be a very long one, but these things are hardly noticeable to the local residents. To a newcomer, however, they may appear odd.

My first course of action was to turn to my young Kazakh driver, Arstan, and ask him for an explanation. Given Arstan's limited knowledge of English and my even lesser understanding of Russian, after attempting an explanation and possibly frustrated at my inability to understand him, Arstan would explain almost everything as follows: "This is the Kazakhi way."

Owing to the language barrier between us, most of our conversations were at first limited to everyday banalities as mentioned above, although with every passing month his English and my Russian improved greatly. My initial questions to Arstan touched upon such things as traffic or why he would automatically address policemen in Kazakh while he spoke to everyone else in Russian.

With our growing vocabulary my questions began to take on more substance, such as when does the ice begin to melt and when does spring finally arrive in Astana? Eventually, as my language skills improved I ventured into the world of politics and culture. His answers to my questions somehow always included the words, "This is the Kazakhi way." Perhaps it was just his way of telling me to stop asking so many questions. It soon became a joke between us that whenever something either made sense, or made no sense at all, we called it "the Kazakhi way."

The Kazakhi way may also be applied to President Nazarbayev's political program. "The economy first, politics second," is the president's mantra. Spend any time in Kazakhstan and you are likely to hear that phrase repeated time and again. It appears to be the president's favorite line whenever he talks about politics, which, as can be expected, is much of the time. But what does it actually mean, the economy first and politics second? In fact it sums up pretty nicely the president's political philosophy and it explains how and why things are the way they are when it comes to domestic policies in Kazakhstan. It is, as Arstan would say, the Kazakhi way.

As to what that phrase actually refers to is really quite simple. Like any president in any country, Nazarbayev has set out a list of priorities for his administration. His philosophy regarding domestic policies is the following: fix the economy and almost everything else will fall into place. Ensure that there are jobs being created for the citizens so that they can put food on the table for their families, and the chances of avoiding social unrest are almost guaranteed.

Once that is done, once the country joins the level of developed nations from an economic standpoint, then and only then can the government begin to think about expanding the liberalization program and allowing the general public greater participation in politics. Presently, it would be political suicide for the country to emulate North American and European democracies. The people are not yet politically mature enough to handle the responsibility that accompanies full-blown Western democracy—assuming that is where the leadership wants to go.

The fact is that Western democracy works well in the West, but will it be the most appropriate for a Central Asian country? It is not a given. The countries of Central Asia are culturally very different from the countries of Europe and North America. In order for democracy to work at its best, it needs to be tailor-made to the individual country's specification. It is impossible to sweep centuries of tradition under the rug and pretend that they are not important.

This may sound somewhat strange to say, particularly coming from someone as ardent a believer in democracy as myself, but implementing instant democracy in the wrong environment can turn around and bite you. Depending on the level of political maturity, sometimes it pays more dividends to spoon feed the people their democratic rights rather than to grant them full rights right away and risk having chaos emerge as a result.

Think of the "economy first, politics second" policy as the pedals of a stick-shift car. The economy is the clutch and politics the gas. When you shift gears you press the clutch all the way down as you remove your foot from the gas. Next you gently lift your foot off the clutch as you start to apply more pressure on the gas. If you do this correctly your automobile will move ahead smoothly and you will be guaranteed a smooth ride. Perform the exercise just described abruptly and the car will lunge forward and you are likely to have either a very bumpy ride or the car will jerk forward and stop suddenly because the engine will stall.

Well, Mr. Nazarbayev's economy-first program is the same. Give the country too much reform without enough economic drive and the system will lunge forward and stall. When you do end up handing more power to the people, you have to make sure that the people you give this fantastic responsibility—the right to vote—do not abuse or misuse their duty as citizens. While voting in most democracies is a personal choice, in a few countries it is mandatory. I don't agree with mandatory voting, but those who give up their right to vote should remain silent until the next election. When you think that some people have given their lives to have the right to vote become universal, abstaining from voting when you can vote is almost criminal.

As you might guess, dinner conversations around our family table when our children were younger often revolved around the political issues of the day. One night our daughter Isabelle, then around eighteen, told us she was going out on a date with a new guy she had just met.

The following day I asked Isabelle how her date had gone and she shot back at me, "He's an idiot. I never want to see him again." My fatherly instincts immediately shot into alert mode. I wondered what this young man could have done to merit that reaction, and I believe as most fathers around the world would do, I began to think of the different ways I could make this man suffer for what he did to my daughter. I asked Isabelle what he had done to deserve her wrath. "It's what he didn't do," she said, "not what he did." And what might that be? "He did not vote in the presidential elections," said Isabelle.

If you give the people too much freedom while the economy is still in progress, chances are you will face social unrest. And when you have social unrest, have no illusions that different groups working to push the flow of events in their favor will be hard at work to destabilize your system. As the case may be, in Kazakhstan as in the rest of Central Asia those forces working to undermine your system are very likely to be *Takfiri*.

Understand this and you understand why the president is holding back on some aspects of political reforms. This issue has come back time and again, raised by human rights groups and Western officials. As Mr. Brzezinski said, the government in Astana has a vested interest in keeping the political climate under control to avoid the sort of outbreaks of violence that periodically grip some of its neighbors.

For lack of a better explanation as to why this country handles Islam in such a silky-smooth manner—so relaxed, so easygoing, and particularly so nonconfrontational—perhaps the answer that makes the most sense, at least for now, would be to say, "this is the Kazakhi way."

This difference of philosophy jumps to mind all the more so when Islam, practiced as it is in other countries, is typically stricter, more rigid, and far more demanding by comparison. Why then is it that this country is at peace with its multicultural, multisectarian, and multiethnic population, when other countries in the region and beyond are facing strife and often violent civil disturbances? As, for example, has been the case in neighboring Kyrgyzstan in 2010.

The "Kazakhi way" may just as well apply to the way the Muslims of Kazakhstan engage their religion. Of the twenty-four Muslim countries I have visited, Kazakhstan is unique in its approach to religion. Indeed, Kazakhstan has opted to follow what certainly is a more liberal form of Islam. The question here is, why? What is it that makes Kazakhstan's outlook on religion as progressive as it is today? And why is Kazakhstan cruising right along in the twenty-first century when many other countries have barely made it past the thirteenth century when it comes to religion? And more important, can the experiment be repeated in other countries in the Muslim world?

There is a misconception among many Muslims that they have to choose between being a good Muslim and living in a modern world. That is wrong, says Radwan Masmoudi, president of the Center for the Study if Islam and Democracy, a Washington, D.C., think tank.

To give a clearer image of what is Islam in Kazakhstan to those who have never been there, a good analogy is to describe the way in which Kazakhs follow Islam by comparing it to the way a great number of French people feel about Catholicism.

The French strongly believe in their Catholic values, their Catholic school education and upbringing and traditions, but at the same time they hardly ever go to church, they disagree with the clergy on almost everything, and they have little time to give the pope; but don't you dare criticize the Catholic Church in their presence.

Kazakhs are much the same. The Muslim portion of the population feels very much Muslim, indeed. They value their Muslim heritage and traditions and are proud that they have withstood the trials and tribulations of sixty years of Communism. But at the same time many Muslim Kazakhs rarely go to the mosque. And much like the French, they hate to hear criticism of their religion.

Whichever adjective you select to describe Islam in Kazakhstan, the bottom line remains unchanged: the manner in which Kazakhstan approaches Islam (and other religions) is worth a more detailed analysis, as it could lend itself as an encouraging example to the rest of the Muslim world to follow in this time of grave geopolitical crisis. That is not to say that Kazakhstan's Muslims are any less Muslim than any other followers of Islam. It is just that they have adopted a different worldview of their religion and of religion in general. Is this a result of sixty years of Soviet influence? Hardly. Other former Soviet republics who were ruled from Moscow for just as long as Kazakhstan have taken an altogether different approach to religion, and to Islam in particular.

Since the 9/11 attacks on the United States, relations between Muslim countries or countries with large Muslim populations and the West have been tense, to say the least. Relations have also been wrought with suspicion and lack of trust between the two sides.

Western governments often suspected—and at times accused—some Arab countries and Iran of fomenting strife in parts of the world and/or supporting terrorism, as is the case with Hezbollah, the Lebanese Shiite organization, and Hamas, the Palestinian Islamic Resistance Movement. Both organizations are regarded as liberation movements by their supporters but are considered to be terrorists by the United States and Israel.

Both groups are heavily funded by Iran, who also provides them with military training and logistical support. Playing devil's advocate for a moment, ask those whom Israel labels as terrorists and they will tell you that Israel practices state terrorism. Just trying to establish the fact of who is a terrorist, or what constitutes a terrorist, is hard enough.

There were, as of a few years ago, 109 different definitions of what constitutes a terrorist, according to Bulat Sultanov, from the Kazakhstan Institute for Strategic Studies. Today there are probably two or three times as many definitions, but still there are no United Nations official definitions of what is a terrorist.

Meanwhile, relations between Kazakhstan and the West have been drastically different from those of many other Muslim nations. Kazakhstan has enjoyed cordial and warm ties with the West, ties that have been free of religious bias or complications. Indeed, Kazakhstan's interaction with the West has been without any major upset, except for the habitual reminders about human rights that Western leaders and organizations feel are something of a necessity whenever they meet Kazakh officials. Regardless, this Central Asian country's relationship with the outside world has been on excellent terms.

Kazakhstan engages in regional security dialogue with ASEAN (Association of South East Asian Nations), and it also enjoys good relations with the Muslim world. It is precisely in this domain that Kazakhstan can be helpful in paving the path to moderation, on the condition that the countries concerned listen and heed the advice that is offered. And this is one battle that is far from being won. Enacting change at that level and on that magnitude from countries and societies will require a monumental effort and a restructuring of the education system. As was mentioned earlier, the answer to the problems facing the Muslim world lies in education and more education.

If tension was gradually building up between Islam and the rest of the world for some time, it reached a climax with the terrorist attacks on the United States in September 2001. The 9/11 attacks have unquestionably changed the basis upon which the West deals with the Muslim world and vice versa. In today's post-9/11 world Islam often finds itself clashing not only with other faiths and cultures, but first and foremost Islam is clashing with itself. Indeed, many scholars, among them John Esposito, argue that this is the real dilemma. The crisis concerns Arab and Muslim nations, where internal social, political, and economic troubles have been reason for concern and have given the Islamist movements a local platform from which to launch their campaigns.

"Modern Islamic social movements and organizations have been the driving force behind the dynamic spread of the Islamic resurgence," says Esposito.[1] Perhaps Kazakhstan's secret is really very obvious and is no secret at all. Is it simply that Kazakhstan lacks the ingredients mentioned above to empower the Islamists? With a large country and relatively few people (fifteen million), unemployment is low, coming in at 6.3 percent for 2010, according to figures from the U.S. Central Intelligence Agency. This is down from 7.3 percent in 2008 and 8.8 percent in 2003.

These figures tend to support the notion put forth by Lisa Anderson, a professor and chair of political science at Columbia University, who states that domestic circumstances typically dictate what sort of Islamist opposition a country is likely to have. "Islamic movements, despite similarities, are the product of local circumstances and conditions," says Anderson. "A failing economy with high unemployment, housing charges and corruption" helps precipitate the growth of Islamist groups.[2]

It would be wrong to say that there is a clash of religions and that the West and Islam are at loggerheads. It is worth recalling that upon the breakup of Yugoslavia it was the West that flew to the rescue of Kosovar Albanians when they were in danger of being overrun by Serbian forces. Kosovo's population is overwhelmingly Muslim, whereas Serbians are Christians. Still, that did not prevent U.S. and NATO forces from defending a Muslim population in the heart of Europe. Today, there are few countries where Americans are warmly welcomed, and Kosovo is one of them. In the capital, Pristina, the main thoroughfare has been renamed Bill Clinton Avenue. Kazakhstan is the other exception.

In the steppes of Central Asia, Islam appears to have found its place among other religions where Muslims live at peace—as Islam calls for—with other faiths. Here, Islam and other religions have found common ground. Why? Perhaps the answer can found in the Kazakh temperament, that of a nomadic people who used to roam the wilderness of these frozen lands by winter and scorching heat by summer. They had to adapt in order to survive. The tough, yet at times welcoming, environment of the Asian steppes has helped the Kazakh people survive the extremes and harshness of the region's elements and over the centuries has even helped fend off invasions from far more powerful neighbors.

Or rather it could be that Kazakhstan, although a large country geographically speaking (it is the ninth-largest country in the world), with relatively few people, is easier to govern. When compared to its immediate neighbors, this is hardly horde enough to fend off the hundreds of thousands of warriors that the Chinese or the Russians could throw at them. And even when they were overrun by outside powers, as they were during the seven decades of Soviet domination, the Kazakhs managed to maintain their sense of hospitality and traditional values. One must not exclude the vital role held in modern Kazakh society by the tribal and clan influence.

Some believe that the hospitable nature of Kazakh society throughout history is at least one of the reasons why Kazakhs are as open to other cultures and religions, and just as important, why they have given such a kind face to Islam. Why then is it that most Muslim countries are struggling to find a workable middle ground between the way they practice their religion and the way they conduct their everyday lives? While some Muslim countries chose to impose their understanding of Islam, Kazakhstan opted for a more open approach to Islam, but a pure form of Islam nevertheless. Kazakhstan has proven that Islam can coexist with modernity and with other religions.

Many scholars, among them Imam Hassan Qawzini, blame the stagnation in Islam on "corrupt governments." "Governments in Muslim countries today, many of which are corrupt, greatly benefit from the absence of *Ijtihad*," said Qawzini. The Iraqi cleric believes governments have ulterior motives for keeping the doors of *Ijtihad* closed because it gives them greater control over the religious establishment. Religious bodies in Muslim countries usually rely on the government to finance their institutions. Some scholars, including Qawzini, believe this makes the religious establishment far too dependent on the government, and Qawzini thinks that if any initiative is to have a chance at succeeding then there should be a real separation of mosque and state.[3]

Why is it then that the leadership in some Muslim countries continues to impose their views of what they believe their religion must be like, rather than let people choose for themselves? Do they believe that they can win in the long run? History has proven that no regime has ever been able to persevere and remain in power when it goes against the will of the people.

Indeed, they can govern for ten, twenty, or even hold strong for thirty years, as have the ayatollahs in the Islamic Republic of Iran. But can those regimes hope to remain in power without their secret police? Once again, one can see the similarity with the Soviet Union. The only thing that held back the people was the Berlin Wall, and it did not resist the will of the people. Similarly, there is a psychological barrier holding back parts of the Muslim world. That wall needs to come down, and that gate, the gate to *Ijtihad*, needs to be reopened.

The leaders of the Muslim world must begin to speak out and take concrete steps to put a halt to the schism between Muslims and the rest of the world. School curricula that incite hatred must be stopped. There is not much of a future in growing up with hate as one's major topic of education.

A pertinent question at this juncture is, why do some religious authorities or political authorities—in some instances the two are one and the same—believe that religion needs to be imposed on everyone in order to be effective? The answer to this question is obvious and was addressed in the opening chapter of this book when I made the analogy between Communism and Islamism. They impose their version of religion because there is no separation between religion and politics. That is the primary difference in Kazakhstan where mosque and state, or church and state, are kept apart as they should be.

Any religion, Islam included, is or at least should be a personal pact between an individual and his or her God. Faith comes from a person's inner body, from the soul. It is meant to be a very personal experience and is not to be shared with or involve an entire community. Indeed, religion should be what the people who follow that religion make of it and not the other way around. Religion is—in principle—about love and forgiveness. Cutting someone's head off because they disagree with your god goes counter to everything that religions teach their followers and what they stand for.

If a religion makes its followers angry, hateful, and pushes them to kill other people, then there is something fundamentally wrong with that religion. "Religion is about love," said Tomash Peat, the Catholic archbishop of Astana. Rather, let me rephrase that thought. There is, of course, nothing wrong with those religions, be it Islam or Christianity. Christians are not immune to accusations of killing based on religious discrimination. Many are those who perished under the sword for refusing to convert to Christianity. What about the Spanish Inquisition? What about the hundreds of thousands who were killed simply because they were in the wrong place at the wrong time?

"There seems to be an inverse relationship between how vociferous believers are in claiming that their religion is peaceful and how peaceful their religion actually is," writes Austin Cline, regional director for the Council for Secular Humanism, a former publicity coordinator for the Campus Free Thought Alliance, and a lecturer on religion, religious violence, science, and skepticism. "Christians can be especially critical of how Muslims keep insisting that Islam is a 'religion of peace' despite the extensive world-wide violence being committed by Muslims in the name of Islam. Such Christians seem to want to insist that theirs is the real 'religion of peace,'" said Mr. Cline.[4]

Yet history has shown us that Christians can be as ruthless as others. During the Cathar War in 1209, in which the Catholic Church waged a crusade against the Cathars in southern France, Arnaud Amalric, the papal legate and inquisitor sent by Pope Innocent III, was asked how the crusaders could recognize Catholics from Cathars as they were about to enter the city of Béziers. Amalric is reported to have said: "Kill them all, God will sort his own."

Centuries later, a similar saying, "Kill them all; let God sort them out," emerged during the Vietnam War. Amalric was also responsible for the mass live burning of "many heretics and many fair women" at Casseneuil, and for the slaughter at Béziers of some twenty thousand men, women, and children in what was termed "exercise of Christian charity." So, let he who is without sin cast the first stone.

The true teachings of the Prophet were not those of hate and did not incite his followers to mindless slaughter of innocents. Rather, the Prophet, who was engaged in a political battle that at the time was a matter of survival for him and his tribe, introduced sweeping new reforms. The survival of Islam is no longer in question here and need not be a matter of concern for Muslim officials. What we are witnessing today in certain parts of the globe is indeed a derivation of Islam for purely political ends.

In the post-9/11 world the international community began to focus on Islam and tried to understand what it stood for. As mentioned earlier, to a large extent what emerged in the immediate aftermath of the terrorist attacks on U.S. soil was a bad case of Islamophobia. Many were those who instantly saw a terrorist behind every Muslim, or perhaps simply wanted to because it was convenient.

And of course some people in politics rode the anti-Muslim bandwagon for all it was worth. Communism was dead, after all, and a new threat was needed to rally the masses. There had to be a "boogey man," a "bad guy" that would play on the emotions of the average American. The United States launched two major wars during the Bush years, one in the Middle East and another in Central Asia—with the backing of the majority of Americans. How was this accomplished when the specter of Vietnam was still fresh in the minds of many? It was done by playing on the emotions of the public, by stressing the fear factor that lies within every individual. Scratch the surface and it's there. In the immediate aftermath of 9/11, with anti-Muslim sentiments running high as they were, George W. Bush could have gotten away with invading the entire Middle East and most of Central Asia, had he chosen to do so.

Regretfully, like false prophets, many false authorities began to emerge from the woodwork, claiming to be "experts" after reading a few books on Islam. Some claimed to understand the intricacies of the religion when many had never set foot in a Muslim land. These experts offered to interpret the meanings of the Quran when Muslim scholars, imams, who had studied the holy book of Islam for decades were still struggling to explain the meaning of a verse or a saying from the Hadith.

With the growing number of nonstop television news programs analyzing and dissecting every political move, the demand for people who could talk on television grew drastically. What ensued was the sudden appearance of hordes of self-proclaimed experts on intricately complex issues. Being an expert on Islamists became something of a lucrative industry. The problem arising from this new—or perhaps not so new—phenomenon is that some people, even some intelligent people, started believing their own rhetoric and that of other "experts."

So now the question that remains is why does Kazakhstan appear to be able to pull it off, while other countries with Muslim majorities are facing serious challenges from within?

One answer is that Kazakhstan has realized what Masmoudi stated at a conference organized by the United States Institute of Peace some years ago, that Islam and modernity can live together.[5] However, for Muslims to become comfortable with the notion and for Islam to accept modernity, the reintroduction of *Ijtihad* is a prerequisite.

We should have no illusions, however, that this road to moderation will be an easy one. Quite the contrary, it will be filled with pitfalls and opposition, some of which may be violent. The guardians of the more strict and conservative form of Islam will strongly object to any attempt to introduce any change in Islam. Instead, they will want to maintain the status quo, as has been the case for the past few centuries.

Ijtihad—or hermeneutics—refers to the institutionalized practice of inter-preting Islamic law (sharia) to take into account changing historical circum-stances and, therefore, brings about the possibility of different views. *Ijtihad* is one of the most important aspects of Islam and needs to be reintroduced. (We will go into greater detail about *Ijtihad* in the next few chapters.)

Strangely enough, it is one of the very little known aspects of Islam. *Ijti-had* is the independent or original interpretation of problems not covered by the Quran, the Hadith (traditions concerning the Prophet's life and utter-ances), and *ijma'* (scholarly consensus). In the early days of the Muslim com-munity, every adequately qualified jurist had the right to exercise such original thinking.

The practice of *Ijtihad*, agree several respected Muslim scholars, "must be revived."[6] In interviews with me, the highest religious authorities in both Turkey and Saudi Arabia have confirmed the need to revive the practice of *Ijtihad*. Additionally, now there is a growing movement among scholars and intellectuals supporting the idea.

Fearing too much change would weaken their political clout, religious scholars closed the gates of *Ijtihad* to Sunni Muslims about seven hundred years ago. From then on, scholars and jurists were to rely only on the original meaning and earlier interpretations of the Quran and the Hadith. Of course it is important to point out that the question of reopening the gate of *Ijtihad* concerns only the Sunni branch of Islam and not Shiites, for whom the gates of *Ijtihad* never closed. The possibility, small as it may be, of an eventual re-opening is of paramount importance to the Sunni world and to the West.

What is a certainty is that if a segment of the Muslim world's population agrees to enact change, and indeed many are those who do want change, the *Takfiris* will resist it with all their might. As a reminder, the *Takfiris* believe in remaining true to the teachings of the Prophet and have resisted change. They don't shy away from turning to violence to achieve their goals. They make no distinction between religion and government because for them it is one and the same, just as it was at the time of the Prophet. Just to clarify a point,

Takfiris are exclusively Sunni Muslims, although Shiites have at various times turned to violence as well.

The *Salafis* are also ultraconservative but differentiate themselves from the *Takfiris* by rejecting the use of violence. In short, all *Takfiris* and *Salafis* are Muslims but not all Muslims are *Takfiris* and *Salafis*. All Muslims who engage in terrorism are very likely *Takfiri* but again not every *Takfiri* is a terrorist. The majority of the world's 1.6 billion Muslims are normal, everyday, decent people who simply want to get on with their lives.

Still, one must not be put off or deterred from pursuing the chance to help bring about change and help create one of the most important dialogues between Christians and Muslims at a crucial time for both worlds.

———

"The prospects could be breathtaking. Considering the degree of pressure now being exerted on the strategic position of the Islamic peoples, there would be a good chance that the main centers of Sunni Islamic learning could reach a consensus that provided all Sunni Muslims with a convincing refutation of the Jihadis' insistence on the religious necessity of armed jihad against the West," writes Pat Lang, a respected writer on Middle Eastern affairs.[7]

Religion in most Muslim countries has a direct impact on almost every aspect of daily life. This is especially so in the Middle East, where the line between politics and religion is blurred and where religion has a great influence on the law. Having said that, it is interesting to note that of the twenty-two members of the Arab world and the fifty-four members of the Organization of Islamic Conference, only two countries—Iran and Saudi Arabia—have sharia as the law of the land. The rest have segments of sharia incorporated into their laws, most of which are based on either French or British law.

———

The effect of a static religion in such a case has had a trickle-down effect on society in general and quite naturally on the way business is conducted, which in turn reflects on how well or poorly a state can conduct and attract business.

According to a 2002 United Nations Development Program (UNDP) report compiled by a group of noted Arab scholars—the first such report covering all twenty-two Arab countries, counting a population of some 280 million people, or 5 percent of the world's population—the Arab world lags behind most other regions in the world. The GDP (gross domestic product) in all Arab countries combined stood at $531.2 billion in 1999, less than that of a single middle-sized European country, Spain ($595.5 billion).

"A telling indicator of the poor level of educational attainment in the Arab countries is the persistence of illiteracy rates that are higher, and educational enrollment rates that are lower, than those of dynamic less developed countries in East Asia and Latin America," states the UNDP report.

The overall educational achievement among adults in Arab countries remains low on average. Arab countries have nevertheless made tangible progress in improving literacy; the estimated rate of illiteracy among adults dropped from approximately 60 percent in 1980 to around 43 percent in the mid-1990s. However, illiteracy rates in the Arab world are still higher than the international average and are even higher than the average in developing countries. Moreover, the number of illiterate people is still increasing, to the extent that Arab countries embark upon the twenty-first century burdened by over sixty million illiterate adults, the majority of whom are women.

By comparison, literacy rates in Kazakhstan hover around the 99.8 mark for men and 99.3 for women, according to a 1999 estimate by the Central Intelligence Agency. The country ranks nineteenth in the world.

Innovation in the main branch of Islam is bound to have a positive effect on the overall lifestyle of the people. It is bound to impact business, education, and the sciences. As Lang reports, the Arab world's "cultural and historic bias against innovation, which has long hampered the economic and political development of the Islamic World, might be affected in a positive way throughout the Sunni world."

The solution to the turmoil gripping Muslim society today may be found in a two-step approach. First is education. There needs to be an overall revision of the public and private education system in the Muslim world. Reopening the gates of *Ijtihad* will allow Muslims "to reinterpret Islam for the 21st century," states a comprehensive August 2004 special report produced by the United States Institute of Peace.[8] Masmoudi believes the process of *Ijtihad* has enabled Muslims to be flexible and to learn from other cultures and civilizations.[9]

The practice of *Ijtihad* must be revived, stressed the same report compiled with the participation of several respected Muslim scholars.[10] Among them were Muzammil H. Siddiqi, a member of the Fiqh (Islamic Law) Council of North America who teaches at California State University and Chapman University; Imam Hassan Qawzini, director of the Islamic Center of America, based in Detroit; Muneer Fareed, associate professor of Islamic studies at Wayne State University; and Ingrid Mattson, professor of Islamic studies and director of Islamic Chaplaincy at Hartford Seminary. These are just a few of the prominent scholars who support the initiative.

Meanwhile, Turkey announced in July 2010 that it supported the idea of reopening the Gate of *Ijtihad*. Today, Muslim society is experiencing turbulence. All peoples, all societies, and all religions go through difficult moments; that is the natural course of life. The challenge is to be able to address those bumps in the road, as it were. A number of events have contributed to the rise of radical Islam: The wars in Iraq and Afghanistan, the continued occupation of Palestinian lands, the frustrations caused by oppressive regimes, and the absence of democracy have all contributed to give fodder to a radical, politicized, and violent form of Islam, whose adherents have turned to terror as a means of achieving their aims. They have, in short, politicized Islam.

Contrary to Samuel P. Huntington's belief that Islam and the West are headed for a clash of civilizations, other scholars argue that the real clash is between two diverging ideas within Islam itself. The clash is between the politicized Islam of a radical element that has turned to violence as a means of expressing itself, and the mainstream majority, which remains largely silent.

"Political Islam has proven a formidable force even though Islamic movements or organizations often constitute a minority of the community," states John Esposito.

So is there hope for a solution to the current dilemma? Yes, there is. As in most conflicts, solutions can only come from within. Similarly, the cures for finding what ails some Muslim communities can only emerge from Islam itself. Resolutions cannot be imposed by the West. But before the House of Islam reconciles itself, two things must happen. First, the Muslim mainstream must play a greater role in its community; and second, it must be given an authoritative tool enabling it to enact positive changes. That tool is *Ijtihad*.

The reintroduction of *Ijtihad* enjoys the support of a growing number of scholars, intellectuals, and Islamic institutions, both in the West and in the Arab world. Even the Saudi Arabian Minister of the Waqf, or religious affairs,

Sheikh Saleh Abdel Aziz al-Sheikh, and Ali Bardakoglu, president of the Diyanet, the highest religious authority in Turkey, support this. Both al-Sheikh and Bardakoglu stated during private interviews with me that they were in favor of reinstating *Ijtihad*.

"The general strategy is to expand the base of 'moderates,'" the Saudi minister told me. But he warned, however, that "so long as there were bad things" happening in Iraq and Palestine, it would prolong negative events in the rest of the world.

Indeed, the roadblocks to *Ijtihad* are numerous and tough. A preliminary study shows that the Muslim world remains divided over who should have the authority to implement *Ijtihad* and how much should be allowed to change. There is no religious hierarchy in Sunniism, the branch of Islam that dominates the Muslim world, as there is in Shiism. Still, the belief is that with time, effort, and education, *Ijtihad* will eventually be reintroduced, allowing important changes to be made. Another hurdle is that historically, reform of Islamic law has often been confused with criticism of Islam itself.

If *Ijtihad*'s doors remain closed and *Takfiri* and *Salafi* influence continues to rise, this will lead to a greater schism between the average Muslim and the radicals, as well as between Islam overall and the West, given that the vast majority of people in the West cannot distinguish between a mainstream Muslim, a *Salafi*, and a *Takfiri*. If this were to happen it would expand the existing conflict, turning it into the infamous 'clash of civilizations,' and it would have severe repercussions for Muslims everywhere, especially those living in the West.

Among the countries concerned by an eventual rise in *Salafi* and/or *Takfiri* activity are the more moderate Muslim countries such as Kazakhstan, Turkey (although some experts will argue that under the leadership of the ruling Justice and Development Party [AKP], the country has already veered into the fundamentalist's camp), Syria, and Jordan.

What is the solution to this dilemma? I believe it is for more countries to follow the Kazakh example and adopt the "Kazakhi" way.

—— SIX ——

Shaking Things Up

"International terrorists do not have religious or national addresses."
—*Kanat Saudabayev, Kazakhstan minister of foreign affairs*

Contrary to popular belief, there have been some changes, albeit very minor ones, taking place in Islam, and they are despite efforts by *Salafi* and *Takfiri* opposition to prevent changes and to freeze Islam in a time warp. In fact what the conservatives in Islam are trying to accomplish is not very different from what conservatives in other religions try to do: keep things as they are without change for as long as possible. The difference is that generally conservatives in other religions do not resort to violence to make a point.

At first glance Islam may seem to be stagnant, especially when compared to other major religions that have adapted at a far better pace to the changing world. But things have progressed, even if ever so slowly.

Indeed the *Salafi* movement has only partially succeeded in slowing down the natural progression of time and trends and the impulse of society to keep up with the changing world. But it would be wrong to say that the *Salafi* movement has been vanquished. It is strong enough and influential enough to have succeeded in slowing down the progress of Muslims in many parts of the world.

This was in part accomplished by keeping the gates of *Ijtihad* closed; however, they have not been able to stop the process altogether, largely due

71

to the progressive vision of countries such as Kazakhstan, who are pursuing their programs aimed at educating their people and promoting understanding between religions and ethnicities. We will return to that thought in a moment.

A major challenge facing most religions today is how to handle the problem of diminishing congregations, with fewer and fewer people attending church on a regular basis. The paradox here is that in spite of the lack of keeping up with changing times, Islam is today the fastest-growing religion in the world. That is the good news for people of the Muslim faith. But before any rejoicing is done it is important to note that the news is not all good. Islam may have the numbers, but the statistics are terribly discouraging. The downside is that according to United Nations reports, the Arab and Muslim countries are at the bottom of the education and productive world social ladder.

The Arab and Muslim world is proud of its many achievements and great contributions to mankind, and rightfully so. Having a rich and glorious past is all very well, but sitting on one's laurels is hardly enough. While it is good for the ego and it looks very good in the history books, it does not help future generations to live in the past.

The Muslim world gave us great theoretical scientists and scientific thinkers. They have contributed to the advancement of the sciences with numerous ingenious inventions that have helped the scientific world discover other all-important breakthroughs. Given the technical means available at the time, these discoveries are all the more astonishing.

Among the inventions credited to Muslims are the telescope (Abu Hasan) and the pendulum (Ibn Yunus), which in turn permitted the measurement of time by its oscillations. The first watch is reported to have been made by a Muslim named Kutbi. Mustansariya, the well-known university of Baghdad, had a unique clock with a dial blue like the sky and a sun that continually moved over its surface denoting the time.[1]

Soap is said to have been introduced by Arab chemists, and Yusuf bin Omar is reported to have manufactured the first paper in Baghdad in 794 AD of a much higher quality than what the Europeans produced. The first observatory in Europe was "Giralda," or "The Tower of Seville," built in 1190 according to the mathematical guidance of Jabir Ibn Afiah.

In medicine, prominent Muslims such as Razi (Rhazes), Ibn Sina (Avicenna), and Abu Ali al-Hasan (Alhazen) were the greatest scholars of their time.

Avicenna wrote *Al-Qanun Fi'l Tib*, known as *Cannon*, one of the most-read medical works of its time. Indeed, the list is as long as it is impressive.

But what has come out of the Arab and Muslim worlds recently? What great contribution to mankind can be credited in the last hundred years to the Muslim world? Have there been any great inventions?

Not a single university figures in the list of the top one hundred schools of higher education in the world. Muslim students seeking quality education in any of these top colleges are obliged to travel and study in Europe or North America.

This dramatic lethargy that has encapsulated the Muslim world for decades needs to change if there is to be any progress as far as closing the gap between Islam and the rest of the world. Again, many of the problems facing Islam today revolve around the issue of education, or rather the lack of it. The West may accept blame for much of what ails the developing world today. Not that it will change much, but the blame can be placed on imperialism, colonialism, and even on Zionism, and part of that blame may even be justified. But when it comes to education the Muslim world has only itself to blame for lagging behind.

From a purely theological perspective it is quite understandable that movements such as the *Salafis* want to preserve their religion in all its grace and splendor as it was founded by the Prophet. But one should be aware that the Prophet lived in a desert climate in the sixth century in Arabia, when the world was an entirely different place. Think how much has changed in the years since the Prophet was alive. From travel to hygiene and from government to business and communication, not much has remained the same.

It is illogical to want to maintain a religion, which is a living system, as it was in a different time era. This would be like someone today traveling from the eastern time zone of the United States to Kazakhstan, where there is a time difference of about eleven hours, but this person would refuse to adapt to the time change and would continue to conduct business on U.S. eastern time.

The redeeming factors are countries such as Kazakhstan that have the vision of what is needed to give their children a better future. At the end of the day, this is what it boils down to: Are we going to leave this world in better shape for our children and grandchildren than the way we found it?

At the initiative of the president, Kazakhstan has made significant contributions to strengthening peace and stability around the world. In the twenty years since the country has become independent Kazakhstan has introduced a number of initiatives aimed at strengthening interreligion and interethnic understanding.

In November 2007 President Nazarbayev invited people of all faiths to accept the Eurasian Charter of Interfaith Peace and Conciliation. In 2003 a major interfaith conference, grouping representatives of all major religions, was held in Almaty, where a declaration of peace was accepted by the forum.

The document stated as follows: "Religions should become the binding element of all civilizations. Peace and prosperity of people is an ultimate goal for all religions and cultures of the world."

Part of the reason for the poor marks on their report card can be explained by the fact that many Muslims live in underdeveloped or in developing nations in Africa and Asia, where historically the levels of education have not fared as well as in the developed world. This is owing to lack of resources, but also to the type of education many Muslims receive in madrassas.[2] A graduate from a madrassa will enter the workforce with an excellent knowledge of the Quran and nothing else. These madrassas are usually set up by an Islamic organization, often, but not always, with funds from *Salafi* institutions.

The idea of the madrassa is a noble one: to provide free education to the underprivileged who could otherwise never afford an education. Quite often the student, or *talib*[3] in Arabic, is housed and fed free of charge, an added bonus and an additional incentive for poor families to enroll their children. So far this is good. The problems begin to arise with the type of education provided to the students, years of studying nothing but the Quran, usually accompanied by extra curriculum centering on hate and rejection of the other. What is being hatched in these madrassas is monumental foundation for greater conflict in the years to come.

In the long run the madrassas are doing a disfavor to the students and to society by producing class after class of students who will go out into a world where the job market is becoming more difficult and where students with double master degrees are having a difficult time landing a job in their field of study. These Muslim organizations would be serving their society in a more concrete and productive manner if they would adopt somewhat broader curricula, other than religious studies. Or rather these religious schools should all be placed under the direction of the country's ministry of education, who in turn should be accountable to an international body such as the United Nations Education and Scientific Organization or the Organization for Security and Cooperation in Europe.

The Kazakh authorities are well aware of the dangerous phenomena and the explosive elements that are gradually brewing in these centers of religious learning. Kazakh authorities remain convinced that the answer is education and they are pushing the issue very strongly. There are a number of madrassas in Kazakhstan and the authorities say they are keeping a close eye on what goes on there. Indeed the Kazakhs have adopted a completely opposing idea regarding the education of their youth. Through a generous state-sponsored program, the Kazakh government will finance the higher education of university-level students in American, European, and Asian schools on the condition they return to work in Kazakhstan.

Through this program tens of thousands of young Kazakhs end up earning a valuable education in the top universities around the world. Besides the obvious benefits such a scheme offers the student and state, allowing the latter a strong and educated pool of workers who will contribute positively to their societies, there are other advantages of this plan.

Students studying in foreign universities tend to develop close relationships with other students, creating strong bonds of friendship. Among those there will without a doubt be some of tomorrow's leaders. This is especially true of the Ivy League schools, where traditionally an impressive number of graduates go on to make a name for themselves in politics. Now compare the life and career expectancy of those young men and women to the opportunities awaiting the graduates of the Quranic schools.

And still, there will be a great number of Muslims, especially those who belong to the conservative branches of Sunni Islam, who will continue to oppose any and all change. Many argue that the last thing they would want is to have their children corrupted by Western decadence. That older generation will remain reluctant to change. That has been the case for several hundreds of years now. The reasons for barring change are multiple; they are historical, they are political, they are religious, and they are cultural. Resisting change is hardly a new trend.

Indeed it is due to a difference of views over who should rule and how they should rule the Muslim world after the death of the Prophet that the great schism between Sunnis and Shiites occurred. This reluctance to introduce change has continued ever since.

The caliphs ruled over politics and religion in what was called a caliphate, where typically the legal system was sharia (Islamic, or Quranic law). The last caliphate was under the Ottoman Empire and ruled from Istanbul, in Turkey. It was often referred to as the *Sublime Porte*. Mustafa Kemal Ataturk put an end to the caliphate on March 3, 1924, after establishing the modern Turkish republic because he believed Turkey's future was more compatible with the West.

One of the fears of the early caliphs was that too much change would weaken their political and religious clout. In more current times, conservatives have generally been worried by modernity. Some go as far as fearing Western culture and norms. They worry that modernity will distract the faithful from the laws of the religion as set out in the Quran. They fear that Western influence will pollute their culture and corrupt their youth. Some of these fears are not totally unjustified.

In a poll conducted by Gallup, Muslims were asked the open-ended question, "In your own words what do you resent most about the West?" The most frequent response across all countries among moderates and radicals was "sexual and cultural promiscuity," followed by "ethical and moral corruption," and "hatred of Muslims."[4]

Modern culture has had a monumental impact on societies around the world. Pop culture, cinema, and television have left their imprint on millions of young people on all continents on this planet. The power of modern culture, be it rock music, the latest fashion trends, or the arts, has revolutionized the world time and again.

Some political analysts credit The Beatles and blue jeans for helping bring down Communism in the Soviet Union and Eastern Europe. And to some extent that is true. Young people behind the Iron Curtain wanted so much to be like young people in the West that they would have done anything to get to where they wanted to go. Look at Western pop music and Hollywood films; despite being banned in some Muslim countries, they are still available on the black market elsewhere.

Of course with the Internet, policing what people watch and what they can listen to has become an insurmountable task. That is not to say that some countries are not trying to control the Web and the access its citizens are permitted.

Popular singers and musicians have been instrumental in helping fight hunger and disease in Africa, raising hundreds of millions of dollars through concerts and specially recorded albums. Popular musicians like Phil Collins, Sting, and Bob Geldof have been successful where governments were practically helpless, ineffective, and inefficient.

Other fears, however, are unfounded and exist only due to the extreme conservative nature of some groups. Ironically, the very elements that helped bring down Communism are now having the opposite effect in much of the Muslim world. In fighting Communism the West helped the countries behind the Iron Curtain to strive for their freedom. The people were encouraged to fight their governments and much aid—a lot of it kept secret—was funneled to them.

Today when fighting terrorism and the threat of terrorism, the United States and its allies are propping up authoritative regimes that they hope will keep the governments in place and the Islamists on the defensive. This policy is one of the principal reasons why there is so much anti-American sentiment around the world.

To cope in a modern, vibrant society, some changes are needed to adapt to an evolving world. Muslims in the United States, for example, are allowed to apply for mortgages in order to buy homes, although usury—the lending of money for financial profit—is forbidden in Islam. In order to be able to live and thrive as most Americans, Muslims needed to be able to buy their homes, and in this case the law was amended.

Resisting change will ultimately leave a negative impact on a society reluctant to move forward with time. That society will in due course feel the pressure of their isolation once economic ramifications begin to settle in. North Korea is a prime example of a reclusive state.

What was said about the political establishment also largely applies to the religious institutions who wanted to retain their influence, especially in the later days when politics and religion diverged to become separate entities in many parts of the Muslim world. Traditionally in Islam the dividing line between religion and politics is a very blurry one to begin with, given that the *Umma*, or the nation of Islam, was first established by the Prophet Mohammad and his political heirs. So, many are reluctant to change because they fear it will change what they regard as part of their cultural heritage.

A majority of the extremely conservative rules imposed on women, for example, are not in the least religious but rather tend to be more cultural in origin. Such, for example, are the restrictions imposed on women and girls by the Taliban, where conservative ideas stem from tribal culture and traditions more than from religious beliefs. The punishment in Afghanistan under the Taliban for women committing adultery, or simply being accused of it, was to be stoned to death in a soccer stadium at halftime. Afghanistan's extremists have banned films, they have prohibited music, dancing, kite flying, and anything that may seem just a tad too entertaining

Yet change and tradition can and do coexist peacefully with religion. We have seen that happen in Kosovo, where the division between religion and politics is clearly marked. Kosovars are proud to have turned down offers from certain Arab countries to build mosques when they first broke away from Serbia. The Kosovars replied that there were sufficient mosques in the country, thank you very much. On the other hand, they said, the money could be put to better use building schools and hospitals, of which the new state was in dire need.

We have seen it in Turkey,[5] where, under the watch of Atatürk, separation between Islam and politics became a shining example of how the two can coexist. Turkey was the first Muslim country to ban the veil for women and the fez for men. Atatürk turned Turkey into a vibrant, modern state and this could not have been accomplished without the strict separation of government and religion.

And we now see the same results in Kazakhstan. President Nazarbayev's efforts to keep religion and politics separated has paid dividends, making Kazakhstan a young and vibrant economic power to be noticed in Central Asia. There is an obvious trend that becomes apparent when countries keep a clear separation between religion and politics. Kazakhstan is the example.

The Kazakhs are well aware of their country's geopolitical situation; its proximity to Iran[6] and only one buffer border from Afghanistan,[7] two countries that, while both have overwhelming Muslim majorities, could not be more diverse, more different, and more opposite of Kazakhstan when it comes to religious understanding. Afghanistan, or rather the Taliban, could serve as the shopping window for conservative Wahhabi philosophy, a country caught in a time warp. But then again, that is where the *Salafis* want to take the country. Add to that the *Takfiri* philosophy that allows the use of violence to address its issues, and the situation becomes critical.

As an example of just how diverse Muslims can be, here is a quick glance at two countries that follow Islam, two very different countries in almost every aspect of the notion: Iran and Kazakhstan.

The Islamic Republic of Iran, an ancient power in the region, straddling Central Asia and the Middle East, with a history and a dynasty that ruled Iran as a monarchy for several centuries. Iran represents the image of Shiite conservatism where mosque and state are intermingled, as indicated by the country's official name. Iran is ruled by a supreme ayatollah who is all-powerful and with whom rests all the authority of power. Iran is one of only two countries in fact where sharia law is in effect.[8] Depending on which end of the conservative spectrum one stands, Iran can either be the model to follow or the example of much of what ails Islam today—the rules of the conservative movement.

Iran is vying for regional power recognition through the use of proxy militias and nuclear armament. The Islamic Republic is arming, training, and financing, as well as giving political support to, Hezbollah in Lebanon, a Shiite movement. For the first time, Shiite Iran is crossing the invisible line that has for centuries separated Sunni and Shiite Muslims and is doing the same for Hamas, the Palestinian Islamic Resistance Movement, which is Sunni. And finally, Iran is pulling all stops to become a nuclear power.

Kazakhstan on the other hand is the very image of the "post-Ottoman Turkey" of Central Asia, and then some. What do I mean by that? Turkey, after World War I and the abolishment of the caliphate by Atatürk, realizing that its future should be closer to Europe than the East, began shifting the country's policies to fall in line with the new thinking. Atatürk, the first president of modern-day Turkey, modernized his country and spared no efforts to separate religion from politics.

One can see a similar approach by Nursultan Nazarbayev, his country's first president and modernizer of present-day Kazakhstan. As much as Iran is conservative, Kazakhstan is liberal in its approach to religion. Religious parties are banned and while Iran is trying to reach out through militias and strong-arm politics, Kazakhstan is reaching out through congresses, assemblies, forums, and other forms of public diplomacy and outreach that sends a message of peace, tolerance, and understanding. While Iran is trying to acquire nuclear technology, Kazakhstan gave it up voluntarily.

If Iran is the face of conservative Islam, then Kazakhstan is the image of what a vibrant, young, energetic, and rising nation should be, attracting foreign investment and businesses from around the world. The people who drafted the Kazakh constitution in 1993 wanted to prevent Kazakhstan from going down the same troubled road as the two countries that are now either in the grip of internal dissent or ruled by a theocratic regime.

Accordingly, the new 1993 constitution banned all religious parties in Kazakhstan. Two years later, the 1995 revised constitution forbade organizations from seeking to stimulate racial, political, or religious discord in the country. Strict government control has since been imposed on foreign religious organizations. As one official in Kazakhstan told me last year, "In the United States you are accused of watching Muslims. We in Kazakhstan watch everybody."

The 1995 constitution, much as its 1993 predecessor, stipulates that Kazakhstan is a secular state, a fact that makes Kazakhstan the only country in Central Asia with a constitution that does not automatically assign a special status to Islam. President Nazarbayev had to choose his course of action carefully, taking into consideration both domestic policies as well as foreign relations.

Too strict rules and restrictions on Islam would have been likely to upset investments from Middle East and Muslim countries, both of whom are big investors in Kazakh industry and trade. On the other hand, too liberal a policy toward religion would be counterproductive for the country's internal security. When asked why Kazakhstan was far more stable than neighboring Kyrgyzstan, for example, Karin from the ruling Nur Otan Party told me that maybe the "control was not so strong in Kyrgyzstan."

Nazarbayev, himself a non-practicing Muslim (who went on pilgrimage to Mecca), does not see his country as purely a Muslim one, but rather sees Kazakhstan as a bridge between the mostly Christian West and the mostly Muslim East. His government is intent on avoiding at all costs Kazakhstan falling prey to Islamist groups. The president has played his cards very carefully. Predominantly Muslim, it is not unusual to hear Kazakhs refer to their religion as "Muslimness":

The Akorda is where President Nursultan Nazarbayev lives and works in Kazakhstan's new capital, Astana. The imposing building stands flanked by other government buildings in what residents of the capital call the New Astana. *Photo by the author.*

A young Kazakh woman walks out of the Glass Pyramid in Astana. Designed by Sir Norman Foster, it contains accommodations for Judaism, Islam, Christianity, Buddhism, Hinduism, Taoism, and other faiths. It also houses a 1,500-seat opera house, a national museum of culture, a new "university of civilization," a library, and a research center for Kazakhstan's ethnic groups. The building is conceived as a global center for religious understanding, the renunciation of violence, and the promotion of faith and human equality. The Pyramid of Peace expresses the spirit of Kazakhstan, where cultures, traditions, and representatives of various nationalities coexist in peace, harmony, and accord. *Photo by the author.*

Two Kazakh women and a child walk in the new section of Astana, where modern architecture overlaps with traditional styles. *Photo by the author.*

U.S. secretary of state Hillary Clinton meets with Kazakh foreign minister and secretary of state Kanat Saudabayev in Washington. *Kazakhstan Ministry of Foreign Affairs.*

Sign of changing times? Traditional "worry beads" hang from a car's rearview mirror. The beads are being replaced by sayings from the Quran and signs with the word "Allah." *Photo by the author.*

A view of Astana's Right Bank, where modern buildings are alongside traditional ones. *Photo by the author.*

Kazakh women shopping. Although Kazakhstan is a country with a Muslim majority, you are likely to find more veiled women in London, Paris, Brussels, or New York City than in Astana. *Photo by Kay Floyd.*

Shoppers in a super-market in Astana can purchase beer by the glass or by the bottle to take home or to enjoy on the spot. *Photo by Kay Floyd.*

Modern architecture retains a hint of old Kazakh style, as seen here in these residential buildings on Astana's waterfront. *Photo by the author.*

No, this is not St. Louis; we are still in Astana. *Photo by the author.*

The Nur-Astana Mosque, meaning "the light of Astana," is the biggest mosque in Central Asia. Located on the Left Bank, the mosque was a gift from the Emir of Qatar, Hamad bin Khalifa. It can accommodate up to five thousand worshippers inside and an additional two thousand outside. *Photo by the author.*

Alina, a Tatar, one of the many different faces that make up Kazakhstan today. *Photo by the author.*

A monument to Kenesary Khan can be seen on the shore of the river Esil in the capital, Astana. Kenesary Khan is increasingly regarded as a hero in Kazakh literature and press. This, however, is a relatively recent trend, since more outspoken views were not possible until Kazakhstan was no longer part of the USSR. *Photo by the author.*

This is intended to reflect the discomfort with the abstraction of an Islam as an ideology and a preference for Muslim life as an experience of the community. Islam, defined by the Islamic theologians, is the ideal, which the community expects the elders to aspire; whereas this idea of "Muslimness" is the religious life of the people, including the elders.[9]

No doubt the control is not so strong in Kyrgyzstan. As Karin pointed out during a conversation in his office in Astana, the mufti[10] of Kyrgyzstan had to be replaced four times in 2010. Two consecutive leaders of all Muslims in the country were kidnapped, and the third disappeared, according to Karin.

There are two quite revealing examples of Nazarbayev's policy on religion. The first was when, as president of Kazakhstan, he made his first pilgrimage to the holy city of Mecca in 1994, but also made sure to include a visit to the Vatican and a meeting with Pope John Paul II. And second, when Kazakhstan was initially invited to join the Economic Cooperation Organization (ECO), President Nazarbayev accepted only observer status. The large majority of ECO countries are Muslim.

To a lesser degree the same can be said of a few Arab countries where efforts are made to separate mosque and state, though historically Arab countries have a harder time separating the two entities than non-Arab Muslim countries. Syria comes to mind as one of the few Arab countries trying to keep religion and politics apart that can claim to have had limited success.

In 2010 the secular-leaning government in Damascus passed a law banning women from wearing the niqab in the classroom. The niqab is the veil that covers a woman's entire face, revealing only the eyes. In doing so Syria became the first Arab country to rule decisively on an issue that has troubled Europeans—and has become an issue of heated debate in numerous European capitals for many years as Europe's Muslim population continues to grow.

Syria's reason for banning the niqab is part of an ongoing struggle by Damascus to fight extremist Islamist groups who, since the 1980s, have been giving the Damascus government reason for concern. Here, once again, I would refer to Professor Anderson's insight as outlined in the previous chapter, where she explains how authoritative regimes empower the Islamists.

With that in mind, it is no coincidence that in the twenty-two countries of the Arab world where Islam is either the religion of state or of the overwhelming majority, and with a combined population of about 338.4 million,[11] the Arab world publishes far fewer books than Spain, with a population of 45 million. The average rate of adult literacy (ages fifteen and older) in the Arab world is 76.9 percent. In some countries the average is even lower, such as Mauritania and Yemen, where the rate is barely over 50 percent, according to a UNESCO report. Women in this region of the world count for about two-thirds of the population.

The average GPI (gender parity index) for adult literacy is 0.72, and gender disparity can be observed in Egypt, Morocco, and Yemen. Above all, the GPI of Yemen is only 0.46 in a 53 percent adult literacy rate. According to a UN survey, in the Arab world the average person reads four pages a year and one new title is published each year for every twelve thousand people.

And if still more proof is needed to confirm those depressing statistics and show that beyond a doubt it is the lack of proper education that is hampering progress in the Arab and Muslim worlds, just compare the Arab and Muslim worlds' achievements and progress in the fields of education, literature, the arts, and sciences to those achieved by other regions in the world with similar demographics, such as Eastern Europe. Emerging from several decades of Communism the Eastern Europeans embraced changes in their society and lifestyles with outstretched arms and open minds. The transformation of the former Eastern Bloc countries was phenomenal.

The Eastern Europeans catapulted ahead, overtaking the Muslim world in just a few years. They embraced the change and recognized it as something that would work in their favor and give their people better futures. Coming from behind, they advanced in light years compared to societies that remained reluctant to change and almost stagnant.

Yet despite the lack of major changes in Islam, there have been some changes all the same: Following the 9/11 attacks on the United States and other terrorist bombings by Islamist groups in Spain and France, Paris pushed hard to get its large Muslim community organized and to have someone speak on their behalf.

There are about four million Muslims in the country, the largest community in Western Europe. The French created an overseeing body to help guide French Muslims, called the French Muslim Council.[12] Jacques Chirac first floated the idea when he was president, and it became a reality under his successor, President Nicolas Sarkozy. The creation of the council in France was a major stepping-stone for Muslims in Europe.

President Nazarbayev in fact had done very much the same thing a few years earlier while he was still first secretary of the Kazakh Communist Party before independence. In 1990 Nazarbayev created a separate muftiate for Kazakh Muslims. Initially Kazakh Muslims came under the authority of the Muslim Board of Central Asia, a Soviet-approved and politically oriented administration overseeing all of Central Asia.

Other, less important changes have also occurred. Consider this important example that separates the words from the actions of the *Takfiris* who claim to reject everything that comes from the West. The Internet.

Officially *Takfiris* shun Western modernity, which some call "instruments of the Devil." However, they have adopted and adapted to the Internet in a major way. The Web has become a favorite tool that is widely used by Islamists of all affiliations to communicate with each other. Militant Islamists use the Web to send encrypted messages around the world.

Creating a personal website is quick and simple to do, if you know how. It literally takes no more than ten minutes to teach a beginner in computers how to set up a very basic site. Hundreds, if not more, of websites are created every day by *Salafis* and *Takfiris* for the specific purpose of communicating securely across the Internet.

Islamist groups, according to several Western intelligence sources, have become proficient at escaping attention of the Internet and are using it to learn how to make explosives and perfect urban guerrilla warfare tactics. There are tens of thousands of pro-Islamist Internet sites online at any given moment. "The Internet is of particular concern," stated Raphael Perl, the head of the anti-terrorism unit with the OSCE Secretariat.

And still conservatives will argue that there is no place in Islam for change. Yet without change the risk of expanding the conflict becomes greater. It is important for the Muslim community, with help from progressive nations and societies who are not afraid to try a different approach in order to solve a very serious problem affecting their community, to scrutinize themselves and to find the answer to their problem. In the final analysis, the solution to the dilemma is to be found from within the Muslim community.

Outside interveners can be helpful in suggesting ideas and gently nudging along the parties concerned, yet the best arbiter in a conflict is someone who at the same time can relate to the problem all while maintaining a certain distance. This is where Kazakhstan comes in.

As a country with a Muslim majority it knows what the issues are from inside, yet a country such as Kazakhstan has been successful in maintaining a certain distance from the turbulence affecting the Muslim world. When Kazakhstan assumes the chair of the OIC in June 2011, it will be in a prime position to launch an intra-Muslim dialogue, on the condition that the proposal is not instantly met with a fierce barrage of opposition from other members who might be more influenced by the conservative movement.

Kazakhstan is the living proof that there need not be conflict between Muslims and the rest of the world. It is one of the most hospitable nations in the world and one of the few countries left in the world where Americans still feel welcomed. In all probability, it is the only country in Central Asia where Americans can travel around the countryside without fear for their safety. It becomes instantly evident when you visit Kazakhstan, where the majority of the people are Muslims who coexist with a multitude of peoples of other faiths. In that regard, Kazakhstan has set an example for the rest of the world to study, to examine, and to follow.

One of the questions that I put forward to almost everyone I met in Kazakhstan while conducting interviews and doing research for this book was the question that first pushed me to write this book: my curiosity as to why, among the fifty-four Muslim countries in the world, is Kazakhstan so different in their approach to religion and their deep understanding of what it means to be tolerant of others.

There was a wide range of explanations, some acceptable, others a polite attempt to reply to something they had no idea about. But three answers I found rather interesting came from three very different people.

The first came from Tomash Peta, the archbishop of Astana and president of the Catholic Bishop's Conference of Kazakhstan. Peta, originally from Poland and now a citizen of Kazakhstan, explains it by saying it relates to the nomadic heritage of the people of Kazakhstan. This, in fact, is something you hear a lot of.

My favorite explanation came from Karin, the secretary of the ruling party who credits a discipline of Islam that I haven't mentioned so far. Karin credits Sufism, a somewhat mystical branch of Islam renowned for its gentleness, kindness, and soft philosophical approach to life in general. Sufism might best be recognized in the West for its famous dervishes, who connect with God by turning in place until they reach an almost trance-like state. Sufism is as far from *Takfiri* as you could possibly get.

According to Karin, a primary reason for his country's different approach to Islam is due to the connection with Sufism. "Islam and our natural approach to Islam can be traced to Sufism," Karin said. "Islam and our natural culture do not contradict each other. Our tradition is in harmony with Islam." Karin went on to explain that in Sufism "there is no mediator between Allah and the people. Kazakhs believe in the spirit of their ancestors."

Aidar Abuov, a professor of philosophy and director of the International Center of Cultures and Religions at the Ministry of Culture, agrees about Kazakhstan's ties to Sufism, but adds two more interesting observations. First, Abuov believes that in addition to Sufism, Islam in Kazakhstan was also influenced by Shamanism,[13] Tangri,[14] Zoroastrianism,[15] and Nestorianism.[16]

Second, the professor of philosophy says that one can draw a clear line from Arabia, where the more traditional—read, *conservative*—Islam had influence, to Tashkent, the capital of Uzbekistan and one of the oldest cities in Asia. From there onward were the Kazakh steppes, where the more spiritual form of Islam influenced by Persia and Turkey had an impact.

The solution to the problems facing the Muslim world, according to Abuov, is to establish centers of Islamic thought and higher learning in the top universities in Europe and the United States where a clear image of Islam can be examined, discussed, and taught. It is through education that this problem will be addressed and hopefully solved.

This can only be achieved through unbiased higher education, the sort of which the Kazakh professor has in mind, not through the thousands of madrassas, places of learning where the credentials the students earn will qualify them to queue up for a spot as a jihadi militant. The madrassas are not the way to build and invest in a nation's most valuable assets, its youth.

Kazakhstan has understood the value of a good education and is investing accordingly. Young people from Kazakhstan are attending the top universities in the United States and in Europe every year. The reality is that much change is needed in the Muslim world in order to allow its young people a fair chance to succeed in a competitive environment. If the Muslim world continues to ignore these harsh facts, the full impact of such a decision will become clear in the years to come. Eventually, they will have to wake up from their political slumber, but by then the world will have moved ahead the next level, leaving the Muslim world trailing behind it yet again. Truth is not always a pleasant thing to hear, but one needs to hear it.

Several years ago I was invited to give a talk at the annual meeting of one of the largest Muslim American organizations in the United States. They asked me to address the issue of Islamophobia, a topic to which I had devoted several columns. I was asked to talk for twenty minutes. During the first half of my speech I said pretty much what was expected of me, and the audience seemed pleased. But then halfway through my talk I shifted gears and told the gathered crowd not what they expected to hear but what I thought was necessary. There were several hundred people in attendance and you could have heard a pin drop.

At the end of my speech the group's director came up to me, looked me straight in the eyes, shook my hand slowly and firmly, and said: "Thank you. We didn't like what we heard, but we had to hear it."

Many of those who might be reading these lines right at this moment might have a similar reaction to that of the people in that large conference hall when I told them of certain realities that displeased them. At the end of the day they were free to take into consideration the information I had shared with them, or reject it. Here, too, I put forward ideas that I judge are for the benefit of those concerned. Similarly, there will be many things said here that they will dislike. But they, too, need to hear it.

SEVEN

The Road to Moderation

"We live on the same earth, breathe the same air, and we are now able to see on television whatever occurs anywhere on the globe. So let us act positively, regardless of our religion and biases, as we are all the children of Adam and have to live together in this world."
—*Sheikh Ahmad Kuftaro, Grand Mufti of the Syrian Arab Republic*

With all the best intentions in the world, the road to moderation is going to be a very torturous and difficult one to pave, and for some, even more difficult to follow. As discussed in the previous chapter, in view of the opposition from conservatives to allow change, one should expect much turbulence and objection from *Salafi* groups. There will be some countries and/or more conservative groups that will refuse to accept even the notion that change is a necessity in order to maintain pace with a modern and evolving society. That is the plain reality. The other issue will be to convince those opposed to change that it is not only a reality but a dire necessity in order to keep Muslims competitive in today's world.

The fear or reluctance to accept change is, in a way, understandable. The main reason people oppose change usually stems from their desire to maintain tradition. Change brings unknown and unpredictable elements into the system,[1] and most people are comfortable within their system and wary of the unknown. But time cannot be stopped and eventually those who oppose change will be faced with this harsh reality: accept the need for change demanded by the natural flow of time or face the consequences. What do I mean by "face the consequences"? Simply this: The Muslim world today cannot live on its own; it needs to interact with the rest of the world community. To do so successfully it needs to adapt, as have other religions. Does this mean that Muslims have to change their customs and traditions? Not at all.

It does mean, however, that the Muslim world needs to revise and scrutinize certain aspects of the House of Islam that have created a state of conflict both within the Muslim world and between certain groups of Muslims and others. It means that at the end of the day those who oppose change will realize that change is an absolute necessity, or else the society as a whole will suffer as a result.

Just as President Reagan asked Mr. Gorbachev in 1987 to tear down the Berlin Wall, so too must those in positions of power in the Muslim world make a landmark decision to reopen the gates of *Ijtihad* and to bring down the psychological wall that surrounds them. Some countries, such as Kazakhstan, are already well embarked on this road to moderation.

Despite their moderate attitude toward religion, Kazakhs feel no less Muslim than others because they have chosen to travel down this path. Still, it will no doubt be a road that will be laden with pitfalls, multiple roadblocks, and strewn with objections from all those who remain afraid of change.

Whoever embarks upon this journey should be prepared to settle in for the long haul because this is a long-term project. Some observers believe it might take as much as two generations, at least, of continuous education, beginning in the preschool level and continuing through high school, before the changes in ideology and outlook on life begins to take hold and to transform the current mindset that is prevalent in some parts of the Muslim world.

Complicating matters somewhat more in the quest to develop and present to the world a milder face of Islam is the fact that this is by no means a "normal" dispute in the traditional sense of the word. It is highly unlikely that this kind of debate will be settled in a series of meetings where one can hope that an agreement will be reached within a specific time frame.

The threat of the conflict escalating, meanwhile, remains very real. "Terrorism is one of the greatest threats to the world," said Kazakh minister of foreign affairs Kanat Saudabayev at a conference organized by his ministry on the topic of curtailing terrorism. The foreign minister said that terrorists used drug trafficking, human trafficking, and other illegal activities to collect funds that are then spent on preparing acts of terrorism, most of them directed at the United States and other Western democracies. However, as the minister and others indicated, Western democracies are not the only targets of terrorists, but so too are other countries in the region.

Terrorist groups, said the Kazakh foreign minister, have attempted to mount a coup in neighboring Kyrgyzstan, while the fighting between those who had mounted the previous coup was raging. "Terrorism in all its forms is becoming a global world threat," said the minister. Another speaker at the same event called it "a large-scale global threat."

How much the moderates will be able to influence the fundamentalists will be the challenge ahead for Mr. Saudabayev when, as minister of foreign affairs, he takes up his position at the head of the OIC in June. Much is going to depend on the approach he takes.

To be sure, Kazakhstan is not alone in its position. There are those in the Muslim world who hope to follow the same philosophy that Astana has adopted for itself and is trying hard to share with any and all who will stop to listen to the message: Islam is not the enemy of the West, and by the same token, the West is not the enemy of Islam. As one can imagine, this is no small order.

Of course this problem will last well beyond the mandate of Kazakhstan's chairmanship of the OIC. In order for all the hard work that Kazakhstan is likely to put in during its tenure at the head of the organization to try and remedy what troubles certain circles of Muslim society today, it is equally important to think about succession to the chairmanship of this prestigious organization. Perhaps a more constructive solution would be to establish a permanent secretariat tasked with the unique responsibility of handling the education dossier in the Muslim world.

One of the very first tasks assigned to this new secretariat would be to establish a working group that would follow more or less the example of the Catholic Ecumenical Councils, such as Vatican I and Vatican II, where the elite of the Catholic Church's clergy convened over a period of several years until they reached a consensus and adopted important resolutions. Here, too, a consensus needs to be reached.

Second, it is through education that we will begin to see the proverbial light at the end of the tunnel. This education has to start at an early age. As an Israeli Facebook friend put it, responding to an earlier report I had written: "I agree with your initial comment that the problem lies within Islam. I have several Muslim friends here in Jerusalem who agree—the problem is in the sort of education one receives at a young age . . . and right now, we have a problem that the PA [Palestinian Authority] is educating young Arab Muslim children to hate and to kill, while Israeli schools teach tolerance and co-existence. So—it'll take more than one or two generations, but we still hope for real peace—what other choice do we have?"

Indeed. At the end of the day there are no other solutions but for people of different faiths to coexist peacefully in order to build a better future for our children and grandchildren. If any single party can broach the question of potential reform in Islam along the lines that we have discussed so far, and do so in a serious manner without the risk of being accused of bias or of holding double standards, it is certainly the Kazakhs.

The Kazakhs have the advantage of seeing, living, and understanding the conflict from all sides. In fact, in this particular case, there are not so much opposing sides as in more "traditional" disputes. Here, there is only one side: Islam. All sides believe in the same religion, Islam, in the same God, and in the same Prophet. The question, therefore, is how some go about interpreting the same word of God, and then implementing the laws of Islam, and then agreeing with those who want to follow the same laws and traditions but see things through a very different lens.

The debate, if and when it gets going, is going to have a better-than-average chance of success owing largely to the role of the interlocutor, assuming it will be Kazakhstan. One reason is that coming from outside the Arab world but being a Muslim country with a large Christian minority, Kazakhstan offers a different perspective to the debate and a better chance of success when the negotiating team is fully aware of the issues.

"Closing the doors of *Ijtihad* is one of the gravest mistakes Muslims have committed," said Imam Hassan Qawzini. "Closing the doors of *Ijtihad* has had extremely detrimental ramifications for the Muslim world." It was a decision that has resulted "in chronic intellectual stagnation," added the Imam. One of the negative effects has been the loss of thousands of potential *mujtahids* and scholars who have been prohibited from offering workable solutions to newly emerging problems over the years.

"Muslim thinkers have become captive to rules that were made long ago, leaving little scope for liberal or innovative thought," said Qawzini. The first step toward opening the door of *Ijtihad*, according to Qawzini, should be the liberation of religious establishments from the influence of political regimes. Religious authorities should dissociate themselves from political regimes so that they can independently issue and interpret religious law.

Kazakhstan, due to its geographic location, is nearly 50 percent surrounded[2] by Muslim countries that either have a strong Islamic presence or where *Takfiris* tend to be active. Kazakhstan, much like other countries in the region has much invested in seeing this tension disappear so that it can get on with the business of making business. And much like many other Muslim countries, especially the more moderate ones, Kazakhstan feels that it must constantly look over its shoulder and remain on the alert for attempts by Islamist groups to infiltrate and divert its society.

The most vulnerable—and the ones typically targeted by Islamist recruiters—are the young men. In many Muslim countries, particularly the ones with strict social rules, where the individual's liberty is in question and where the local authorities decide what is and what is not permissible for an individual, the Islamist recruiters' job is facilitated by the boredom of the people. That, however, is hardly the case in Kazakhstan, where in view of the country's liberal attitude young people are free to mingle and go to clubs, movies, and restaurants, and to socialize with members of the opposite sex as they see fit.

During my stay in Astana I was told by several young Muslims that they were approached by foreign Islamists while praying at the mosque during the Friday noon prayers. They said these foreigners tried to convince them that they should adopt more outwardly Muslim signs, such as growing a beard and giving up alcohol.

No doubt Kazakh security forces, reputed to be very much on the ball, are keeping a watchful eye on any Islamists in the country, as a matter of routine. As one high-ranking government official told me once: "In the United States you tend to watch Muslims. Here in Kazakhstan we watch everyone."

While Kazakhstan has been thankfully immune from terrorist activity so far, Kazakh officials have admitted that there have been attempts to "involve our citizens in terrorist activities." Still, according to officials in Astana, Kazakhstan is not fighting terrorism, but rather the threat of terrorism.

The government of Kazakhstan hosted a meeting of leaders of the world's traditional religions in Astana last year where the issues of tolerance and education once again arose, the latter brought to the forefront of the agenda by Monsignor Khaled Akasheh, desk officer of the Section for Islam of the Pontifical Council for Interreligious Dialogue at the Vatican. In an interesting sideline to the meeting, which included a rabbi from Israel and a representative of the Islamic Republic of Iran, as the leaders gathered for the opening session they all shook hands or hugged. But when Meir Danini, the representative of the Sephardic Chief Rabbi of Israel entered the room, Mozaffari Mohammad Hossein, the director of the Center for Interreligious Dialogue of the Islamic Culture and Relations Organization from Iran, avoided crossing looks with the rabbi.

When I later asked the rabbi about his interactions with the Iranian representative, he explained the ground rules. The Iranian representative is allowed to dialogue with Israel's representative during working sessions, and he is also allowed to exchange looks during working sessions, but, the rabbi explained, the representative of the Islamic republic is not allowed physical contact with the Jewish representative. No handshake. The rabbi did not appear upset by the discriminatory rules imposed on a meeting of religious leaders, where there should be no ground rules.

This conflict is not really a conflict in the traditional sense of the word, where there are two or more sides involved in a dispute over territory (land, borders, or water rights) or over politics (to have a greater say in the governing of the country, greater political clout, and a larger share of the political pie). Rather, this conflict involves religion. And when one involves God in any debate, particularly when one is convinced that God supports *his* point of view, that *his* truth is the only truth, and that there should not even be a debate over the issue, the conflict becomes all the more explosive.

One example that comes to mind is an experience I had several years ago when I was asked by a nonprofit organization to set up a short course in Gaza for Palestinian journalists on the ethics of journalism. I raised the issue of truth in reporting and said that a journalist must always report the truth. However, I cautioned, there is not necessarily one truth; there are various aspects of the truth. There is what one person will interpret as the truth and then there is what another sees as the truth, and quite possibly there may be a third truth: the real truth. Both sides are convinced that they know the truth; they stand their ground; and the conflict escalates.

As Friedrich Nietzsche, the famed German philosopher, is quoted to have said: "You have your way. I have my way. As for the right way, the correct way, and the only way, it does not exist."

The Palestinian students seemed utterly confused. How can there be more than one truth, they asked. It is precisely this issue, I pointed out, that is the basis of every conflict, when all sides are certain that truth is on their side. Now add God, and you see the complications amplified expeditiously. Still, one needs to remain optimistic and persevere, because in the final analysis there can be no other solution; there is no other alternative. Either the Muslim world takes care of its internal affairs through mediation and dialogue and more countries jump on the Kazakhstan bandwagon, or an important segment of the Muslim world finds itself on a collision course with the West, and the end result could lead those countries of the Muslim world to become as economically stagnant as the Soviet Union and the Eastern Bloc used to be.

That would be disastrous on a number of levels, most of all on the economy of the countries concerned. As President Nazarbayev keeps repeating when pressed about democratic reforms and human rights, "the economy first." A stable economy is the foundation of a vibrant and economically healthy society. In turn that translates into a content population that becomes ready for greater democratic reform, and the society at that point becomes more politically mature and less apt to turn to violence as a means to settle their problems.

As in most conflicts, viable solutions can only come from within if we want to increase the chances of success in any negotiation. An outside negotiator helps the procedure along, particularly when that intervener can exert pressure on the parties concerned. For example, the manner in which the United States can exert pressure on Israelis and/or the Palestinians in the neverending Middle East peace process is one form of this.

And yet, in spite of the monumental prestige and influence that comes with the backing of the White House and the Department of State, not to mention the backing of the United Nations, the European Union, and Russia, no final agreement has been reached in the Middle East because the two parties directly involved are not fully convinced that they should make concessions. And that is a vital element in any negotiation.

Indeed, the United States can nudge, bully, and sweet talk the participants to the negotiating table, as can any viable interlocutor. But ultimately, it is up to the stakeholders to reach an agreement. No one can force two opposing parties into closing a deal unless they really want to. Much in the same manner the solution to what is troubling Muslim communities can only emerge from those communities themselves. No Western protest is ever going to make a difference. Resolutions, just as solutions, cannot be imposed from the West or even from other Muslim countries or parties.

Kazakhstan, however, will be in an excellent position from which to exert its influence when it assumes the chair of the OIC in June 2011. At that point, Kazakhstan will have the added benefits and prestige of the organization to add to its own prestige when becoming a facilitator of dialogue between Muslim communities around the world. Kazakhstan will find itself in a far better position to develop its views regarding religion and, more specifically, to portray to the international community that there is a gentler and kinder face of Islam that can live in peace and harmony with the rest of mankind. Kazakhstan will also at this time find itself in a far better position to impress upon its fellow Muslim nations that there exists a viable alternative to an open conflict with the West.

There are four basic steps that need to be taken in order to prevent future negotiation from failing. First, listen attentively to what the other side is saying. This means to truly and without reservation or interruption listen to every word said by your opponent.

It sounds easy, but you'd be surprised at how many negotiations fail because one side was not able to allow others to finish their presentation without interruption. Listening in this context also means making an effort to understand the concerns of the other parties involved. This means to try and understand, truly understand, what are the wants, needs, and fears of the others, and to see their problems through one's own eyes. One does not need to agree with what is being said, but one must understand the other side's perspective without reservations or prejudice.

Second, remain at the negotiation table no matter what the other parties may say and no matter how provoked one may feel. This is often the crucial point in any negotiation, when one is often tempted to stand up and storm out instead of having to endure the diatribe from the other party. As the saying goes, one does not negotiate peace with friends but with enemies. In this context the two sides are not enemies per se, but when discussing religion tempers can flare very easily.

Third, and this is perhaps the hardest part of trying to guide Islam toward the road to moderation, is to convince mainstream Muslims that they must play a more proactive role in the community in which they live and work.

Muslims can no longer be bystanders in today's world. Muslims must get involved through their local cultural centers, associations, and mosques. Left to their own devices, these places become centers of recruitment by the extremists. Naturally this is easier said than done. We know the extremists will not hesitate to use violence. What is an honest man or woman to do if confronted by extremists? Alas, the answer is not very much. Going to the local police is usually a waste of time, as more likely than not the police will file a report and leave it at that.

Perhaps one solution would be to set up a website where people in the community can establish an online dialogue with a special organization created exclusively for the purpose of advising individuals on the proper procedures to follow, without placing themselves and their families in the line of danger.

And fourth, Muslims wishing to implement reform should not be frowned upon by the rest of the community, rather they should be encouraged and helped in any way that they can be helped. Muslims must be given an authoritative tool enabling them to enact positive changes that will lead to better understanding within the community and between the community and the exterior. That tool, of course, is *Ijtihad*. The body whose job it will be to try and initiate the acceptance of *Ijtihad* can very well be the new secretariat.

There is hope today that the movement to reintroduce *Ijtihad* garners greater interest among intellectuals and scholars in the Muslim world. Somewhat unexpectedly, given their conservative streak, Saudi Arabia, speaking through its minister of the Waqf, supported the idea of reviving *Ijtihad*. Sheikh Saleh Abdel Aziz al-Sheikh confirmed this much in a private interview a few years go in Riyadh. Similarly, Ali Bardakoglu, president of the Diyanet, the highest religious authority in Turkey, supports this notion and has written extensively on the issue.

Both al-Sheikh and Bardakoglu are very important figures in the Muslim world. Their support of *Ijtihad* needs to be utilized by the negotiators in any future debate. Saudi Arabia is the bastion of conservative Islam, and Turkey, until recently at least, represented the progressive branch of Sunni Islam. What needs to happen now is for every prominent Muslim in favor of *Ijtihad* to come out publicly and announce their support of the motion.

Yes, the roadblocks to *Ijtihad* are numerous and difficult to overcome. Despite earlier reports indicating otherwise, serious studies have shown that the Muslim world is still far from convinced of who should have the authority to implement *Ijtihad* and how much should be allowed to change. Still, the belief is that with time, effort, and education, *Ijtihad* will eventually be reintroduced, allowing important and necessary changes to be made.

An interesting aside is how little is known about *Ijtihad* in the Muslim world. Mention that word around a group of Muslims and you are likely to get quizzical looks from many.

Numerous are those Muslims who are unaware of the potential power *Ijtihad* may have in helping resolve the intra-Muslim conflict. No doubt many are those who will think that it is outright blasphemous merely to suggest that there may be some internal dissention within the House of Islam. Conservative Muslims have at various times labeled those who have attempted to introduce reforms as unbelievers.

Fatwas, or religious edicts, have even been issued against potential reformers, at times condemning them to death. This hurdle is real and will require Muslims to see the difference between critiquing Islam in order to tear it down, and reforming Islamic law in order to build up Muslims and their societies to a better future.

No doubt many will raise their voices in protest against suggestions that changes are needed in order to avoid any further escalation or dissent, and many are those who want the status quo to remain.

The real courage lies in introducing change. This is what *Ijtihad* is all about: bringing change to religion in order to keep it moving along as society changes over the decades. There is still much that is ignored about *Ijtihad* in the Muslim community, let alone in the international community. Some confuse it with the word *jihad*, or holy war, and the etymology is the same. But *Ijtihad* is the opposite of jihad. It is intended to bring about positive change, not strife.

However, change often brings conflict, of a sort, and that concept worries many. But conflict, when managed and moderated, is not necessarily a negative thing. A vibrant society needs conflict; this is what motivates people. A society without conflict is a dead society. Again, the challenge is to control the flow of the conflict to keep it manageable.

This brings us to the following point, one which Kazakhstan has been active in, particularly since this Central Asian country was named as the rotating chair of the OSCE: mediation. No sooner had Kazakhstan been named as the head of the OSCE than the country's foreign minister began traveling around the Caucasus and Central Asia hoping to find peaceful solutions to long-running conflicts. Kazakhstan's leadership very quickly understood the importance of conflict avoidance and management.

To every conflict there is a solution. That at least is the theory. Eventually that should also apply to the Middle East conflict, which in turn is feeding into the problems troubling Islam and the West, and by default the rest of the Muslim world. The real challenge facing the peacemakers in a conflict is to identify the right solution for the conflict at hand. This may seem to be a rather simple formula to what has always been a complex problem. Kazakhstan's task of ushering in changes, in what has been a stagnant dossier for centuries, will be rendered a tad easier once it has the ears of the other fifty-six members of the organization.

Efforts were made by the foreign minister to use his country's influence and of course the prestige of its leadership. Further efforts will be made by Kazakhstan to help bridge the growing East-West divide, once it assumes its newest position as the head of the OIC in June 2011. Historically, reform of Islamic law has often been confused with criticism of Islam itself. Still, there is a bright spot to close this chapter on a positive note. Even before assuming the chair of the OIC, Kazakhstan pushed forward a resolution condemning terrorism committed in the name of Islam. Big accomplishments begin with baby steps.

——— EIGHT ———

Islam and Modernization

"The majority of the world's Muslims do not believe that terrorism is
a legitimate strategy or that Islam is incompatible with democracy."
—*Gijs de Vries, former EU counterterrorism chief*

W ill the real Islam please stand up and be recognized? There has
been much confusion, mainly in the West, as to who or what
represents the true face of Islam—and with good reason. For the
uninitiated, it would be hard to understand all the different schools of thought
of the different groups that make up Islam. Most Westerners assume that
the religion is the one they hear the most about, the one that makes the Six
O'Clock News. But it isn't.

Is Islam represented by the violent streak that has been so prominent since
the 9/11 terrorist attacks on the United States and subsequent attacks on
London, Madrid, Mumbai, Istanbul, and so on? Is it the Islam of Osama bin
Laden and the Taliban, who do not hesitate to turn to violence to settle their
differences? Is it the Islam of the extremists, the *Takfiris*, who beheaded innocent victims on tape and then posted their gruesome work over the Internet
for the world to witness their cruelty?

Or is the true face of Islam the gentler, kinder, and more pragmatic side
of the religion one finds when talking to the multitude of Muslim leaders one
meets at some of the interfaith conferences organized by the Kazakh government—Muslims who come across as men of peace, such as Derbisali Kazhy
Absattar, the Grand Mufti of Kazakhstan, for example?

Mufti Absattar was kind enough to take time between two speaking engagements and another interfaith conference to share some of his thoughts with me on a number of relevant issues touched upon in this book.

First and foremost, the mufti agrees with the concept that there is no conflict between the West and Islam. "Absolutely not. The people in the West who believe that Muslims are all terrorists do not know the true face of Islam." The mufti, who is the highest Muslim religious authority in the country, said that when a Japanese terrorist places biological agents that kill people in the Tokyo subway, he is not referred to as "a Buddhist terrorist." "The people who commit acts of terrorism have no God."

Mufti Absattar is of the opinion that the conflict is indeed one within Islam, pitting the *Salafis* against the rest of Islam. The head of all Muslims in Kazakhstan admitted that his country was a secular state, that it was not a religious country, but that religion has a major role to play in helping solve conflicts. As to what was the best solution to solve the current crisis within Islam, his reply was education: teaching Muslims that there should not be any animosity between the House of Islam and the rest of the world. "In the final analysis, Muslims, Jews, Christians, others, we are all from the same God," said the mufti.

The words of the mufti of Kazakhstan should serve to reassure those in the West who still believe there is a terrorist hidden inside every Muslim, just waiting to strike at them. But then again, will these words be enough to assuage the fears of those suffering from Islamophobia?

The concept of Islam to the majority of people living in the West has been largely tainted by the tragic events of September 11, 2001. For many Westerners, the explanation of what is Islam is simplified to the lowest degree: total ignorance prior to the 9/11 attacks and general misconception post-9/11, with many believing that most Muslims are terrorists and that the West is now at war with Islam.

That, of course, is wrong. The vast majority of Muslims are not terrorists and the West is not at war with Islam—despite claims by some "experts" who profess to know the real intentions of all Muslims. Much of the knowledge that many Westerners have of Islam is limited to less than the basics, which is not very much to start with. And the fault is not all that of the West. With the exception of efforts by the Kazakh authorities to initiate a valid dialogue between different faiths and different religions, the "traditional" Muslim world's response to the 9/11 attacks has been dismal.

I recall a meeting I attended in Washington, D.C., shortly after the attacks, where a Saudi Arabian delegation composed of political and religious officials were going to engage in open discussions with a panel of journalists, on which I had been invited to participate. We looked forward to the event, as up until that moment there had not been any feedback from the Saudis. The debate got off to a bad start when some of the Saudi representatives accused the American press of being at fault for the anti-Muslim sentiments in the United States following the attack. Instead of sharing information, as we hoped they would, they went on the offensive and in the end several journalists simply walked out. Not the best attempt at public relations.

Sadly, this may explain, in part, why Americans—and Westerners in general—know so little about Islam, except for the most negative aspects that have a way of surfacing on their own. The little that is known about Islam comes from media reports that are often biased and/or erroneous. The negative side of Islam, the ugly side, populated by terrorists and suicide bombers, regretfully has dominated the headline news practically on a daily basis since the 9/11 attacks in 2001. Many Americans remain convinced that Muslims want to dominate the world and force everyone else to convert or die.

Alas, arguments by those who tend to know the more realistic face of Islam are shattered with every new bomb attack in Kabul, every suicide bomber in Baghdad, and every threat of greater pending disaster. "Those people who plant those bombs in Baghdad and Kabul are not real Muslims," the mufti stated.

Indeed they do not represent the true face of Islam, but they represent Islam nevertheless, which is why it remains of primary importance for the Muslim community to speak out and aggressively denounce those who are hurting the image of Islam. The actions of a handful of fanatics have tarnished the reputation of millions of honest people. Every time an official who happens to be a Muslim lashes out at the Jews, for example, threatening the destruction of Israel, it only reinforces the notion in the minds of Westerners that Islam is on the warpath.

There are no doubt Muslims who would like to see the world turned into one big Islamist caliphate, stretching from the Pacific Ocean to the Atlantic

Ocean and even beyond, where sharia is the only law and where there is no tolerance of any sort for others. I believe Osama bin Laden is one of those people, and I believe there are still a number of Islamist groups out there who would like to see this dream become a reality. But those are not the true believers of Islam.

"Radical Muslims do not speak for Islam. Terrorists and extremists are not Muslim," commented Bawa Jain, one of the speakers at one of the numerous interfaith conferences held in Astana last October. So, who does? There is no single supreme position equivalent to that of the pope in Sunni Islam. There is no supreme ayatollah as in the Shiite branch of Islam. Talk to any number of Muslims about the events that have unfolded since September 11, 2001, and they will tell you without hesitation that extremists have hijacked their religion.

What is clear in any case is that there are multiple facets to Islam and each is very different. When you talk to experts in the field of religion, be they men of the cloth or politicians or just people with an interest in religion, they will tell you that there is a very distinct and very visible difference between the Islam influenced by the Arab world and the Islam influenced by Eastern philosophies.

When I asked an adherent of Sufism if he was Muslim, he replied, "What is a Muslim? Someone who surrenders to God? Then yes, I surrender to God." There ought not be such a difference between Muslims, as in essence there is only one religion called Islam, which means "surrendering to God." Being a good Muslim means total surrender to the goodness of God.

For the Sri Lankan philosopher of Sufism, Bawa Muhaiyaddeen, "True Islam means cutting away all hostility within ourselves up, embracing everyone in brotherhood, uniting congregation with congregation. We must remember that all the children of Adam will become one congregation on the Day of Questioning, in heaven, in paradise, in the kingdom of Allah. Everyone in Islam must remember this. If we all accepted and understood this, we would not fight."[1]

The difference between mainstream Muslims and the extremists is cause for serious concern, because it touches upon a very important factor that until now seems to have been largely swept under the rug. Traditionally, ordained representatives in a religion, be they Christian, Muslim, Jewish, Buddhist, or from any other religion, have more or less a similar function. Call them priests, bishops, pastors, sheikhs, imams, rabbis, monks, shamans; it makes little difference, because in essence their roles are more or less the same. The job of these men and women who have devoted their lives to serving God has traditionally included acting as intermediary between God and the people. The people speak to the middlemen—the clergy—who in turn relay the message to God, through prayer.

But what the Islamists are doing is attempting to turn the tables around and to purport to be speaking to the people *for* God. That is a very big and very dangerous development, because if it is allowed to continue unchecked, where does one draw the line at what "God" may say or command when speaking through the voices of the extremists?

At what point will the people begin to realize that God is not talking through these mortals, but that they are ad-libbing for God. We can now understand why it is of paramount importance first to enact changes that would put a stop to such behavior, and second why when we talk of introducing change in Islam, those who remain vehemently opposed to that possibility are precisely those who stand to lose the most if there were ever to be any reform introduced.

Whether or not reform is eventually introduced remains to be seen, but in the interim there are other tasks that can be achieved with the help of governments and groups in a position to influence the parties concerned, such as the work being carried out currently by Kazakhstan.

Under the direction of the country's president, Kazakhstan has launched a number of initiatives aimed at bridging the gap between different religions, and stressing the need for tolerance and understanding. "Many people can come here and learn from Kazakhstan," said Rabbi Yeshaya Cohen, the chief rabbi of Kazakhstan. "Other countries should follow the example of Kazakhstan."

Over conversation that lasted several hours, as part of the research conducted for this book, with a number of religious leaders in Kazakhstan that included representatives from the Catholic and Lutheran churches, the Jewish chief rabbi, and the grand mufti of Kazakhstan, all admitted to the uniqueness of Kazakhstan when it comes to handling religion.

Just what is it that drives the Kazakh government, a secular government, to become so deeply involved in trying to mediate in two of the world's most precarious issues: terrorism and religion-based divisions among peoples, which in turn has led to terrorism?

The answer lies in the understanding by Kazakhstan's leadership that just as religion is a force that has led to conflicts among people because it touches their very soul, that very same religion can be used to counter any negativity emanating from that religious source. The expression "fighting fire with fire" comes to mind, but instead we should be fighting religious intolerance with religious tolerance.

Kazakhstan finds itself today in a unique position to be the perfect moderator of interfaith and intercultural dialogue, given its Asian affiliation and its deep relationship with the Western world, given its deep understanding of both Western and Eastern cultures and ways of thinking, and given that there is a single word that best describes the Kazakhs and places everything in perspective. That word is "Eurasia."

Eurasia, a combination of Europe and Asia, is a short but effective word that summarizes and adequately describes the state of mind of this most unusual country. Eurasia is Kazakhstan, or is it the other way around? Is Kazakhstan Eurasia? Kazakhstan is a country that is geographically situated in Asia but mentally, emotionally, and geopolitically is beyond Asia as it is beyond Europe. Basically, what this means is that while in terms of geography Kazakhstan may be situated in Asia, the Kazakhs do not consider themenselves Asians the way Chinese, Japanese, Malays, or Koreans do. While Kazakhs feel a certain bond to Asia, they tend to look more toward Europe, where they have a strong bond that was established by the Russian (Soviet) presence for more than sixty years. Yet at the same time they realize they are not European, either.

Kazakhstan is the new up-and-coming kid on the political block; it is the wonder kid with new ideas for a better future. Kazakhstan could have chosen to remain out of the limelight, had it not believed in what it is trying to accomplish for the benefit of all nations and all people.

With oil now flowing at a steady pace and filling the state coffers with hard currencies, with a population of just over fifteen million people in a country four times larger than Texas, and with a fairly stable economy given the overall state of world markets, Kazakhstan could have opted to remain on the sidelines of Central Asia's political scene. It could have concentrated all its efforts and resources worrying about its own politics and religion, leaving all the problems that come attached with such issues affecting our world today for the larger powers to fret over.

There is a reason why Kazakhstan is involved the way it is. If the United States sometimes sees itself as the world's policeman, with an urge to jump into a fight in order to try and right some of this planet's wrongs, then Kazakhstan sees itself as the conscience of the world with an urge to preempt and prevent the wrongs from happening in the first place.

However, cognizant that in today's global village it has become nearly impossible for any country, large or small, modern or ultra-conservative, Muslim or Christian or Jewish, to recluse itself from the rest of the world and hope to continue to conduct business and trade on a competitive scale.

There is even a lesson here for the Communist world from the Kazakhs. Now here is an interesting comparison, Kazakhstan and North Korea. The two countries may share the same Asian heritage as well as the onetime belief in Communism, but that is about all the two countries could ever expect to have in common. If North Korea is the world's most reclusive state, Kazakhstan is among the most welcoming. If North Korea has chosen to remain in its corner and continue efforts to acquire nuclear weapons, Kazakhstan's foreign policy has been diametrically opposite, involving itself in every major issue of importance in the world today.

During a single week last October, Astana played host to a meeting of the Congress of Leaders of World and Traditional Religions, and the Conference on Successful Strategies to Prevent Terrorism. Both were high-level meetings with participants from around the world flying in to attend, with active input from the Kazakh organizers.

Why this ardent preoccupation with religion and terrorism? Because during the last several years both issues have come knocking on the doors of Central Asian republics, and Kazakhstan, for one, wants to make sure that they are not allowed to sneak in through the window.

A few people, including many of the so-called experts that the counterterrorism industry has spawned during these past few years, have often wrongly placed all Muslims into a single group. Not only is this approach wrong from a number of views—practically, morally, and functionally—it also can be detrimental to the security of the United States and the Western world. Kazakhstan has been very fortunate in being spared the predicaments suffered by some of

its neighbors. Besides the trouble in nearby Afghanistan, Kazakhstan's secu-
rity apparatus is keeping close tabs on next-door Uzbekistan, Turkmenistan,
Tajikistan, and Kyrgyzstan, who are burdened by a serious problem related to
Islamist extremism.

Although the two countries do not share a common border, the Kazakhs
are particularly worried by the situation in Afghanistan, where the country
has been in the grips of a ferocious civil war on the one hand, and fighting
the *Takfiri* and their allies from other Muslim countries, but primarily from
the Arab world who in the past were more actively supporting the Taliban. A
number of Saudi Arabian princes, for example, were secretly funding *Takfiri*
groups in Afghanistan, even after the Soviets were ousted. That does not mean
that there are no potential terrorists in Kazakhstan. Kazakh officials describe
some of the people they are keeping under close scrutiny as "some extremely
dangerous people from certain Arab countries."

When I asked the mufti if there were any *Salafis* in Kazakhstan, he replied
that there may be "a few," but that they were certainly not Kazakh. "They may
be from Saudi Arabia."

That is exactly the type of situation the Kazakhs want to avoid, allowing
the proliferation of Islamists that can begin to recruit Kazakh youth. If *Salafi*
elements do manage to infiltrate the country, and if they manage to circum-
vent the security service, they will quickly realize that they will have a hard
time recruiting followers. Certainly they will have a harder time than in Arab
Gulf countries. Why? Because for the most part one joins up with such movements out of revenge or out of sheer frustration in regard to the social and
political situation in the country. The vast majority of Kazakhs do not fall
under that category.

This is another area where the leadership showed outstanding foresight
and was being proactive in order to be productive. The president's policy is
that if the economy is stable and doing well, the rest automatically falls into
place. When the people have jobs and when they are well fed, there will be no
reason for them to turn to violent politics or to seek answers in politicized religion. The proof is in the pudding, as the saying goes. Look at countries that
practice democracy (i.e., countries in North America and in Europe), where
there is no fear of violent politics, no fear of coups or revolutions. That is prin-

cipally due to a stable economy, despite all the problems that the industrialized nations face, such as unemployment and corruption.

Remember what Professor Anderson said in an earlier chapter about the triggers of politicized Islam and the fact that it usually finds root in situations of strife. The Kazakh leadership is all too aware of the dangers that militant Muslims can bring to a country and the havoc they can create. With that in mind, we begin to better understand the thinking behind "the economy first" maxim and the intense efforts undertaken by the government in Kazakhstan to address the economy before going on to internal politics. If the economy works, everything else falls in line.

Accordingly, Kazakhstan has taken the lead in Central Asia and beyond in geopolitics, economics, and religion. And in each field there are multiple stories of success. Let's take a quick look at politics first. From the outset, Kazakhstan has demonstrated clear thinking and a coherent domestic economic policy, as well as a sound foreign policy. Kazakhstan made history in January 2010 when it took on the chairmanship of the OSCE during what President Nursultan Nazarbayev called "an era complicated by the global financial crisis and tectonic shifts taking place in the global order.

"The erosion of the regime of non-proliferation of weapons of mass destruction, terrorism, humanitarian and ecological disasters, famine, poverty, epidemics, reduction of energy resources, conflicts on interethnic and interreligious grounds, such is a far from complete list of challenges faced by the modern civilization requiring maximum efforts of reputable multilateral institutions like the OSCE," said the Kazakh president at the time. Since its independence from the Soviet Union twenty years ago Kazakhstan has made a real contribution to strengthening regional and global security. The leadership made a number of quick but nevertheless paramount decisions concerning nuclear weapons. While some countries are pursuing ambitions to become nuclear powers, Kazakhstan has gone the other way.

Since breaking away from the Soviet Union Kazakhstan has shut down the Semipalatinsk nuclear test site and voluntarily renounced its position as holder of the world's fourth-largest nuclear and missile arsenal. At the behest of Kazakhstan the U.N. General Assembly has adopted a resolution proclaiming August 29 the International Day against Nuclear Tests.

Since then, Kazakhstan found itself in an ideal position to mediate between East and West and between the Christian and Muslim worlds. Together with other OSCE member states, Kazakhstan fully supported efforts aimed at bringing the East and West together in order to develop better understanding of the key issues of the modern world. As Nazarbayev said, "The multi-ethnic and multi-religious composition of our population is a special trait of our country. Representatives of more than 140 nationalities and 40 confessions live together as one big family in Kazakhstan."

———

On the economic front, Kazakhstan is somewhat comparable to Abu Dhabi in the early 1970s, at least that is what is often heard from veteran businessmen and diplomats in Astana. There is something of the booming UAE years in today's Kazakhstan. Replace the below-zero temperatures of Kazakhstan's long winters with a warmer climate, and the comparison becomes more realistic.

There is one major similarity between Kazakhstan and the United Arab Emirates, and that is the oil. Kazakhstan's proven oil reserves, according to a 2009 report issued by the U.S. Energy Information Administration, are estimated at thirty billion barrels. The country has the second-largest oil reserves among the former Soviet republics after Russia, as well as large natural gas reserves.

———

Kazakhstan's oil industry is still in its infancy when compared to other large oil producers. But once fully developed, production from the country's major oil fields could place Kazakhstan among the world's top five oil producers, along with Saudi Arabia, Iran, and Russia. This could happen within the next decade.

Steadily rising natural gas production is turning Kazakhstan from a net importer to a net exporter in the near term. Natural gas development has lagged behind oil owing to the lack of domestic pipeline infrastructure linking the western producing region with the eastern industrial region. The most comprehensive list established by the U.S. Department of Energy places Kazakhstan in fourteenth place in the list of leading world exporter of oil. The latest figures available (at time of printing) were for the year 2009, with Kazakhstan producing 1.54 million barrels per day, of which 94 percent was crude oil. The country has proved reserves of 30 billion barrels.

When plans to further develop its giant Tengiz and Karachaganak fields are executed, production will increase by some 1.5 million barrels per day by 2014. Additionally, Kazakhstan's Caspian Sea fields are believed to hold several other major oil and natural gas deposits. Those are still unexploited and are far from their full capacity. On the economic front, you have to remember that while the country's current financial report is less than perfect, given the state of every market from Atlanta to Seattle, or as the people over at the OSCE like to say, "from Vladivostok to Vancouver," Kazakhstan's GDP is by far superior when compared to other nations in the region.

"You see many immigrants in our country from neighboring countries," said a Kazakh schoolteacher. "They come here as low-paid day laborers. They are from Uzbekistan, Tajikistan, Turkmenistan, etc. They will do the jobs that no one else in Kazakhstan is willing to do." She continued, "When you travel to those countries, you see the same type of projects, with the same types of people. One thing that you do not see are Kazakhs in that crowd. That means that our economy is strong and sturdy. That means that our president is doing something right."

You hear similar reports from other people. Even those who openly criticize the government and the president, accusing him of human rights violations, admit that there is something good going on in Kazakhstan. When asked why she would vote for the president after all these years, a young voter explained that it's because the president kept the economy sound and the country strong and safe. And she added, "I don't want my country to be like those around us."

And as for religion, Kazakhstan has paved the way toward new horizons. Astana's vision of religion is giving hope to both the Muslim world and the West that there need not be a conflict between the two civilizations, nor should there be reason for strife in the Muslim community. The question at this juncture is if anyone will have the courage needed to follow on that long—but much needed—road to moderation. No doubt many are those who will criticize attempts to bring about change, as are those who will attempt to obstruct it. The challenge will be to persevere and not be discouraged.

——— NINE ———

The Kazakhstan
Experiment

"He who is deprived of gentleness is deprived of good."

—Prophet Mohammad

When the Soviet Union packed up and left Central Asia in 1991, it left behind a great political void, along with much uncertainty as to what the future of the region would hold. At that point there was no telling what would happen to the countries Moscow had granted independence. Would they remain Socialist? Would they veer to the right? Would they remain in their current state or would they plunge into civil war? Would they break up into smaller entities, as was the case with the former Yugoslavia?

In all cases the answer was "unlikely," given their cultural past and their present religion, Islam. Of all the former fifteen Soviet republics, only Kazakhstan had so many different minorities, nationalities, and ethnicities.

The other four Central Asian countries—Kyrgyzstan, Tajikistan, Turkmenistan, and Uzbekistan—have high Muslim majorities. In the Caucasus, Georgia and Armenia are nearly 100 percent Christian. Azerbaijan is Muslim and the three Baltic countries, Estonia, Latvia, and Lithuania, as well as Moldova, Belarus, and Ukraine, are predominantly Christian.

Moscow hoped to retain some influence over the former Soviet republics by creating a Confederation of Independent States (CIS). That agreement was probably not worth the paper it was written on. For most of these countries

111

that were once an integral part of the Union of Soviet Socialist Republics, the future was now in question.

There was no precedent for what had happened, there was no past to judge by and no telling what the future would hold once the dust had settled. It was a very unnerving time for the people of the former Soviet Union. Yet at the same time these were very exciting times, as people knew they were living through some historic moments.

The only certainty in these very exciting, yet deeply troubling, times was that nothing was certain. All the cards were on the table and everything was up for grabs. The sudden departure of the Soviet Union from the region allowed for unknown forces—which, until this moment, had either remained dormant or were nonexistent under Communist rule—to surface. Certainly nationalism emerged within some of these republics, giving way to clashes and riots with ethnic minorities in their countries, as was the case in Kyrgyzstan last summer when Uzbeks were targeted.

One of the most active forces to make its appearance on the post-Soviet Central Asian scene was of course militant Islam, Islamism, or the *Salafi* tendency that typically manifests itself politically more so than the quiet and peaceful wing of traditional Islam. Indeed, the *Salafis* were already on their way to becoming an active force in Central Asia, even before the last Soviet soldier jumped aboard his transport.

That may be true of most Central Asian nations where Islam is a dominant factor in the former Soviet republics, except for Kazakhstan. Astana opted for a very different approach. The government of President Nursultan Nazarbayev reacted very differently to the situation than its neighbors. The government in Kazakhstan secured its borders; rid the country of weapons of mass destruction, and the immeasurable responsibility that comes with having nuclear weapons in one's territory; gave priority to fixing the economy, which was in shambles; and placed much emphasis on internal security, with particular attention being given to Islamist movements who were active outside the country. Kazakhstan made certain that religion remained where it should be and as it should be— that is, available to all those who want it in the manner that they want it, and not something that is forced upon the people regardless of their beliefs.

Religion in Kazakhstan is optional, it is respected, and it is expected to be respectful of others, whether they are religious or not. And, as an afterthought, religion is expected to remain out of politics. Inside Kazakhstan, religious parties are banned by the constitution. Kazakhstan is and wants to stay a secular state where there is no state religion.

The question of religion aside, Kazakhstan also realized that its future was in aligning itself more with the West, while at the same time keeping its ties with Moscow, which remains a dominant force in Central Asian affairs, and with which Astana enjoys cordial relations.

When U.S. forces invaded Afghanistan shortly after the 9/11 attacks, a number of countries offered military assistance to the United States. Washington's initial reaction was to say thanks, but no, thanks; we can manage on our own. The general opinion from inside the White House at that time was that U.S. troops, with their undisputed air superiority, better-trained and -armed soldiers, and unmatched electronic intelligence-gathering capability, would oust the ragtag Taliban with their limited arsenal, along with their al-Qaida acolytes, in a matter of days.

Well, once again, not everything went according to plan and the United States was forced to rethink its options. Still, the United States was not all wrong; they did oust the unholy alliance rather quickly. But what the Americans and their allies ended up with was basically Kabul, and even then it remained far from secure.

It just as quickly became obvious that the task proved to be far more difficult than initially expected. It also became evident that the United States could not manage the conflict entirely on its own, especially once the war in Iraq was launched and troops and matériel had to be diverted there because it took priority. So Washington began turning to the international community for help. Many countries replied positively to Washington's plea for assistance, realizing the threat posed by al-Qaida and its followers. Among those countries to answer the call from Washington was Kazakhstan.

Astana reacted quickly to the U.S. appeal for help and as a first step allowed flights over its territory by coalition aircraft engaged in the war effort in Afghanistan. This was more of a symbolic move, a politically astute gesture on the part of President Nazarbayev. It was intended to send a message to Washington that Astana was supportive of the war on terrorism and cognizant of the perils lurking in the neighborhood that were directly related to the war on terrorism.

In purely military terms, Kazakhstan's offer, though helpful, had very little importance because the vast majority of air operations in Afghanistan were run out of Kazakhstan's neighboring countries from bases in Kyrgyzstan, Tajikistan, and Uzbekistan. But as an added gesture Kazakhstan dispatched a team of liaison officers to the U.S. Central Command. The U.S. war effort in Afghanistan would not have suffered had Kazakhstan chosen not to open up its airspace to the allied pilots, but it was an important political move.

What was important here was not only the message of support that Kazakhstan wanted to send to Washington, but it was also a message to the immediate region and to the destabilizing forces who might have considered "investing" in Kazakhstan. That message was, "Don't even think about it." Astana would not tolerate any trouble and religion would not be an issue.

As Kazakh foreign minister Kanat Saudabayev mentioned when I interviewed him in early January 2010 in his office in Astana, "Terrorists are terrorists." The minister did not like to use the term "Islamist terrorists," as was widely in use in the Western media. For the foreign minister and for many others I have spoken with in Kazakhstan, the religion practiced by the terrorists is irrelevant in this context. "Terrorists are terrorists regardless of their religion," the minister insisted.

Kazakhstan also understood very quickly the potential damage that terrorists (be they Islamist or otherwise) could cause to the area. Still, Kazakhstan's awareness of the threat from militant groups, regardless of their religious affiliations, has come to the forefront of Astana's policy of international cooperation.

Just as the United States realized it could not set the world straight on its own, Kazakhstan understood—and tried to get other countries to understand—that the new threat to world stability, and more particularly to the stability of Central Asia, was a battle that necessitated close cooperation between the countries concerned. And in this case every country was concerned and remains concerned by the potential spread of this new world threat.

For Kazakhstan the reality of the danger from these militant groups was too close to home. In Kyrgyzstan Islamist militants made inroads in the country's Batken region in 1999. There were bombings in Tashkent, believed to be the work of militants from the Islamic Movement of Uzbekistan in 1999 and 2000. Some of these incidents led Kazakhstan to strengthen its border defenses and begin looking at the problem and core issues of the conflict and what to do about it.

———

At about this time al-Qaida was being routed from Afghanistan in the aftermath of the U.S. invasion and Osama bin Laden was out looking for new bases in the region—as well as new allies to replace the Taliban. The newly independent countries of Central Asia were ideal for al-Qaida. Even though not many support the *Takfiri* movement, nevertheless they are Muslims and they allow for other Muslims to blend in and pass unnoticed.

Strange alliances formed when Islamists began to flirt with organized crime. They started to make lucrative deals with drug traffickers and prostitution rings, strange bedfellows indeed.

The Islamists found they could raise money much faster, and a heck of lot more of it, if they facilitated the passage of several tons of opium, rather than waiting outside a mosque for handouts from the congregation after Friday noon prayers.

Kazakhstan decided it should take a proactive role in attempting to solve the intra-Muslim dilemma, rather than wait around for the other shoe to drop—and what better vehicles to deliver this message than the chairmanships of the Organization for Security and Cooperation in Europe and the Organization of Islamic Conference? Indeed, when Kazakhstan assumes the rotating chair of the OIC in June 2011, it will be in an ideal situation to transmit its message of moderation to the rest of the Muslim community, and of course the chairmanship of the OSCE allows it to do the same.

Being one of the few success stories emanating from the post-Soviet zone in Central Asia, Kazakhs know that unless they are able to bring the rest of the region into *their* zone of influence, there are good reasons to fear that they would be dragged into the others' zone of influence, and that would be disastrous.

Speaking about the former Soviet Central Asia states on September 25, 2010, in a discussion held at the Johns Hopkins School of Advanced International Studies, Dr. Ariel Cohen said that when it comes to that part of the world, "The survival of nineteenth-[and] twentieth-century-style nation state is in question." He was referring to Tajikistan and Kyrgyzstan.

Dr. Cohen, a specialist on Central Asia with the Heritage Foundation, continued, "Kazakhstan is a nation state and you can make a plausible case that Kazakhstan is the most successful state in the region, to wit, the multi-directional energy export pipelines, to wit the chairmanship of the OSCE, etc."

————

There is also another imminent danger looming on the horizon, and it is one that concerns Kazakhstan probably more so than any other country in the region. That new threat comes from what is likely to happen in the region after the eventual pullout of all U.S. forces and their equipment, and the race for domination of the region.

You may ask, "What does Kazakhstan have to do with any of this? And where does Islam factor in here?" Kazakhstan is directly concerned by an eventual U.S. withdrawal from Central Asia, and as we have seen, Islam plays a big role and intends to play an even bigger role—but not if Kazakhstan can help it. And Kazakhstan *can* help it, and it is doing so successfully for the time being. But just as the departure of the Soviets created a void, so too will the withdrawal of U.S. forces.

Here is a frightening thought, and one which no doubt must have more than one Kazakh official losing sleep over it: Should the United States eventually decide that it has had enough of Afghanistan, declare victory, and leave, we could be standing on the doorstep of ominous developments, not only for Afghanistan but for Kazakhstan as well.

Dr. Cohen again: "That would create a power vacuum in that part of the world with a trans-national factor, a trans-national, radical, jihadi-style Islam, not having a counterbalance." The United States learned the hard way what happens when one actor does not have a counterbalance, as was the case in Iraq. When Saddam Hussein's regime was removed and there was no counterbalance, Iran stepped in and its power and influence rose.

"If the U.S. and the allies leave Afghanistan, will this situation be contained?" Because, "if, God forbid, the Taliban take over in Afghanistan, what will be the repercussions on the five states of post-Soviet Central Asia?" Dr. Cohen, as many other Central Asia specialists do, subscribes to the old "domino effect" theory that was so prevalent in political analysis of Southeast Asia during the Vietnam War, and he believes that the domino effect could play itself out in Central Asia.

In Central Asia the fear is that if the Islamists manage to establish themselves firmly in one country in the region, then it would only be a matter of time before they would spread to the rest of the region. In essence, what this means is that unless radical Islam is contained in Afghanistan it could very well make its way to the rest of Central Asia. Think of the consequences of such an eventuality! With extremist Islamists in control of Central Asia, and with virtually unlimited funds collected through some of the largest oil fields in the world, there is no stopping their advance. Indeed, as Dr. Cohen said, unless the Afghan crisis is managed properly, we could be on the brink of "an ominous time."[1]

Hoping to prevent such a turn of events from becoming a reality is yet another incentive for Kazakhstan—and the other former Soviet republics—to promote and encourage the gentler, kinder face of Islam.

We have seen this gentler and kinder Islam take hold in Kazakhstan, but is it possible for the Kazakh model to be copied and repeated in other parts of the world, be it in Central Asia or the Middle East? That is far from being a given. What makes the Kazakh experiment of governance so interesting is in fact the great insight and belief the leadership has in conflict avoidance. This is neither white nor black magic. It is simply intelligent analysis, which in turn is acted upon in an intelligent manner.

While the world's fastest-growing religion is perceived in a negative light in much of the Western world, Kazakhstan has no hang-ups or problems with identifying itself as a Muslim country, while still being at ease with itself and the West.

Kazakhstan is still very much a Muslim country. But if you come here expecting to find a traditional Muslim society, the sort of place that has been on the nightly news bulletins for the past ten years, you will be terribly disappointed. The traditional body wraps and headscarves and conservative dress codes adopted in many Muslim countries is a rarity in Kazakhstan. You will see more of those in Paris, London, and Berlin than you will in Astana, Almaty, or any other city in Kazakhstan.

Muslims still identify themselves as such, but it is an approach to Islam that is relaxed and at peace with itself. There is a saying in English that "if you can't beat them, join them." Except in this case there is no joining them; it is simply not an option. In Kazakhstan's case it is more likely to be along the lines of "if you can't make them join you, then beat them." Kazakhstan understood that military might alone was not going to solve the problem.

Part of the U.S. problem in Afghanistan, as well as that of the allies, is that they cannot sustain this war indefinitely. The costs will eventually weigh down on the economies of the allied countries, and at some point, some politician running for office who is trailing in the polls will make a promise that should not be made. In sheer dollars and "sense," think about how much it costs to maintain a single U.S. soldier in Afghanistan.

Forget the meager pay of the average infantryman, an E3 or Army private (about $19,746 per year), but for every infantryman, there can be six to ten support personnel providing essential supplies, support, and intelligence to keep that one soldier operating. For example, much of the potable water used by the sixty to seventy thousand U.S. troops in Afghanistan is trucked in from somewhere else, either from Uzbekistan or from locations within Afghanistan. That requires logistics and transportation on a massive scale.

For transportation alone, imagine what it must cost the U.S. military to fly seventy thousand troops to a theater of operations and then have to rotate the troops in and out as they take leave, finish a tour of duty, begin a tour of duty, take a short R&R break in Europe, and so on. Not to mention the cost of flying all the military matériel to and from the sites they are needed.

On the other hand, as former Pakistani president Pervez Musharraf told me about two years ago, "All the Taliban fighter needs is an onion, a loaf of bread, and an AK-47 to keep him going, while the United States is overequipped." The Taliban also have no time constraints or elections to worry them.

Short of using tactical nuclear weapons to wipe out suspected Taliban strongholds, along with vast segments of the local population—obviously not a good idea—a purely military victory is not in the cards anytime soon. That does not mean the war cannot be won; it can, but it will take more than sheer military power. The war can be won with the active participation of the international community, but more important, the war can be won if the root causes of the problem are addressed.

Bin Laden's strategy is to continue to force the West to spend billions upon billions of U.S. dollars to maintain troops in faraway stations, until the cost eventually catches up with them. While maintaining military pressure on the Islamist rebels in Afghanistan is important, it is just as important to realize that victory and peace will be achieved only by rebuilding the country's infrastructure. Fighting terrorism necessitates a two-pronged approach—a military approach and a humanitarian angle—in order to secure victory. On the military side what is required is the basic form of action by special forces and smart intelligence. Covert action is absolutely central to winning the war on terrorism, just as it was the decisive instrument of the Cold War, said a senior U.S. intelligence official.

Covert action remains a critical instrument in the war on terrorism, and it is thanks to a number of covert operations that the United States, according to a high-ranking Pentagon official, has made headway in the war on terrorism.

But there is still a long way to go and real threats to counter, particularly as the Afghan insurgency has gotten significantly more intense in the past two years.

On the humanitarian front the constructive and positive line to follow would consist of preempting the Islamists in an area where they are traditionally stronger and where they inevitably make points with the populace. What makes the Islamists powerful and what endears them to the people? It is their ability to demonstrate that they care for the common people when governments are inactive or incompetent.

Let's look and see where the Islamist groups are most powerful. Where are their biggest successes? Where are the Islamists most popular and where could they win an election, if fair and free elections were to be held?

The strongest and most influential Islamist parties other than the Muslim Brotherhood in Egypt, which is an institution all by itself, are the Shabab in Somalia, the Taliban in Afghanistan, Hamas in the Palestinian territories, Hezbollah in Lebanon, and multiple parties and factions in Iraq and Pakistan, as well in some of the "Stans."

What does this tell us simply by looking at these locations? The answer is quite simple: The Islamists, especially those with armed groups, such as the Shabab, Hezbollah, and Hamas, do very well for themselves where there is either a failed state or a weak government. Somalia and Afghanistan are examples of failed states. Lebanon, Iraq, and Pakistan are examples of weak governments.

The same applies to the former Soviet republics of Central Asia. Where there are weak governments you have a strong Islamist presence, and where there is a strong central authority, such as in Kazakhstan, there is no noticeable Islamist presence.

What is the lesson to be learned from this exercise? If I were a politician I would conclude that strong governance that provides the basic necessities for its citizens such as security, prosperity, and basic services such as child-care facilities, health-care facilities, banking facilities, and dependable emergency response services, would not find the urge to turn to an Islamist organization for assistance.

This is the case in both Lebanon and Gaza, where the state is either very weak or nonexistent. What results is that the Islamist organizations, such as Hamas and Hezbollah, step in offering their help and services to the citizens of the territory. There is a catch, however; these services come with a price. The price can be either to request votes when election time comes around or to request that citizens join the party and/or the militia to defend their demands.

In countries where the state provides all the basic services, the Islamists would have no reason to exist, and those groups that did would be much weaker. Typically, many of the Islamist groups are composed of three branches. The first is the traditional political party that can be part of the political process in the country, such as Hamas in the Palestinian territories. The second branch of many Islamist parties is the social services branch. They will step in where the government is nowhere to be found and provide things such as child care, health care, and so on. The third branch is usually the armed elements of the party.

What typically gives the Islamists their strength is the popular support they enjoy. Take that away and their morale and recruitment targets will fall considerably. There is one caveat: the assistance offered must come from the heart and be given with compassion, humility, and civility, and not be thrown at the feet of those who need it.

The war in Afghanistan, for example, will never be won militarily. Here is a perfect example of how the West can score points. When Pakistan was hard hit by an earthquake some years ago, entire villages were left stranded as winter approached. Thousands of people were abandoned with no help in sight.

I remember writing a column at the time stressing the importance for the

Western allies to ensure that aid and assistance arrived rapidly to those who remained stranded in the snow. I wrote that it was of paramount importance that aid arrives before the Taliban descended from the mountains and offered the surviving men a pair of sandals, a blanket, an AK-47 assault rifle, the equivalent of $300, along with a loaf of bread and an onion. That was a golden opportunity for the alliance to mark some points with the people. Who do you think got there first?

The tribal areas of western Pakistan remain the most significant strategic threat. However, the threats do not only emanate from traditional Muslim lands. According to a high-ranking U.S. intelligence official, those threats "can emanate out of the United Kingdom and other parts of Western Europe, too."

According to Michael Vickers, an assistant secretary for special operations and low-intensity conflict at the U.S. Department of Defense, if you look at the number of terrorist threats over the past decade, you would see as many or more coming out of Europe as the greater Middle East.

Vickers believes that al-Qaida's goal remains unchanged. They hope to catalyze an Islamist insurgency, to break up and/or prevent the formation of international military coalitions arrayed against it, to exhaust and expel the West from Muslim lands (as they attempted to do in Iraq), and to overthrow what they consider illegitimate states and establish a new caliphate.

They seriously intend to weaken the West and transform the international balance of power to favor this new caliphate. "Rather large ambitions, to say the least," said Vickers.

But despite these dark predictions all is not dire, as U.S. and allied intelligence services have earned their keep and have scored major points in the war on terrorism. Some of these successes have been quite significant.

In looking back it is obvious that not all the five former Soviet Central Asian republics will be able to follow the successful example of Kazakhstan. One major challenge will be to try and repeat the Kazakh success story in other parts of Central Asia. As an experiment in nation building, Kazakhstan has proven that it is on the right track. Yes, it is still far from being a shining example of democracy, but then again, is there such a thing as the perfect country, the perfect government, or the perfect democracy?

Of the scores of people that I have interviewed while gathering information for this book, from foreign diplomats, religious leaders, scholars, famous actors, and the odd journalist who has ventured this way to the Kazakh Steppes, all are unanimous in voicing a similar thought: the future for Kazakhstan looks bright.

What has been achieved in just twenty years since independence is truly an amazing and impressive accomplishment. Kazakhstan has built a vibrant modern society that is now an example for others to follow. The road to full democratization is a long and painful one with many speed bumps along the way. It is not a superhighway that one can travel overnight. The pertinent question now is, can the present experiment be duplicated and exported?

There are numerous factors that come into play in making Kazakhstan a success that other countries in the region might have a hard time emulating. First and foremost is the mentality of the country. If that could be bottled and exported it would generate greater income than the country's oil production.

———

Traditionally I remain wary of opinion polls that give a head of state an overwhelming approval rating. Having covered regions of the world where such items as opinion polls can be easily manipulated, I rarely trust them or their sources. But when it comes to President Nursultan Nazarbayev's approval ratings, it is an entirely different matter.

It's not that I think the Kazakh president is not likely to move decimal points around in order to give himself an added edge, it's that, having lived in Kazakhstan for several months, I don't believe he needs to do that.

I know it's hard for Westerners to believe that a president in a developing country can be a popular figure, especially in a country where there have been reports of abuses of human rights and a clamp-down on the press. But one really cannot judge from Washington, Paris, or Brussels. One needs to see firsthand why Nazarbayev is liked.

The first thing that Kazakhs will tell you is they compare their country to the four other "Stans": Kyrgyzstan, Tajikistan, Turkmenistan, and Uzbekistan. And what appears when you compare the standard of living of Kazakhs to their neighbors, when you compare the levels of unemployment of Kazakhs to the other countries in the region, when you compare the number of immigrants who arrive in Kazakhstan from the other countries looking for work (tens of thousands) to the number Kazakhs who travel to neighboring countries looking for work (zero), speaks volumes.

A poll conducted in 2010 placed the president once again at the top, and the one thing that Kazakhs mentioned the most was stability. This Kazakhs came to appreciate even more after Kyrgyzstan underwent months of violence that included a coup that ousted the president and ethnic strife that broke out into utter confusion and mayhem and the deaths of hundreds of people.

The greater the violence was, the more the Kazakh president was appreciated back home. "The main thing [for the public] is that the ruling power in the country should be very strong, one which will provide people with order, calm, peace, and an absence of the upheavals we are observing in the neighboring country," Gulmira Ileuova, head of the respected Strategy Center of Social and Political Studies, told a news conference in Almaty in August. Eurasianet.org reported in its August 17, 2010, edition that the study that polled 1,592 people nationwide in July 12–20 showed that 89 percent of Kazakhs are satisfied with Nazarbayev's work. This represents a 4 percent increase since the previous poll conducted in February. The 89 percent mark is not surprising, as typically the president's ratings hover around 90 percent.

There is a genuine political opposition that ran against Nazarbayev in the last presidential elections and lost. But having lived in Kazakhstan I can attest that the president is genuinely popular among his people, and even those who will criticize him will admit he has done a lot of good for the country.

The ethnic unrest in neighboring Kyrgyzstan in 2010 was an eye-opener. Yet Kazakhs were split as to the causes of the April uprising that forced President Kurmanbek Bakiyev from office. The Eurasianet.org study showed 21 percent believing the event was a "popular democratic revolution," 35 percent thinking it was the result of a power struggle between political clans, and 32 percent seeing it as simply the latest in Kyrgyzstan's ongoing political crises; 12 percent were unable to determine a cause.

The fighting next door was largely due to the dismal economic situation in the country, something that once again reinforces Nazarbayev's vision of fixing the economy first.

──── TEN ────

The Terror Threat and Reasons for Concern

"The terrible thing about terrorism is that ultimately it destroys those who practice it. Slowly but surely, as they try to extinguish life in others, the light within them dies."

—*Terry Waite, former British hostage in Beirut*

There are two aspects to the problem of terrorism in Central Asia. The first is the concern governments in the region have for terrorism, and the second is the concern they have for the threat of terrorism. Those are two quite distinct concerns. The first is in the present tense, where there is cause for actual danger from existing terrorist organizations and imminent threats. The second concern is a potential future threat that may well materialize unless something is done about it before it is allowed to mature into a full-fledged terrorism problem. It is the latter problem that has Kazakhstan worried.

Not all countries in the region are affected by terrorism but all countries are affected by the threat of terrorism. Most terrorist groups in Central Asia are motivated by religion, and with little exception, most are Muslim groups. There are non-Muslims fighting in support of various causes around Asia, but these do not concern Central Asia.

And while the Central Asian terrorist groups are believed to have close links with Osama bin Laden's al-Qaida organization, at least the Sunni Muslim groups, for the most part they have remained geographically limited to their

125

country of origin. Unlike al-Qaida they have not gone pan-Islamist, concentrating instead on a single location, as for example in Uzbekistan.

The Central Asia terrorist organizations will cross international frontiers, but that is owing to the fact that for logistical and operational reasons they need to base themselves in a separate country to avoid capture.

"Terrorism in Central Asia is a cross-border phenomenon, with most of the terrorists active in Central Asia operating out of Afghanistan," claims Martha Brill Olcott, from Carnegie, in a testimony prepared for the U.S. Congress Committee on International Relations, subcommittee on the Middle East and Central Asia, and titled "The War on Terrorism in Central Asia and the Causes of Democratic Reform."[1]

Most Central Asian experts will agree that the region is a hotbed of Islamist militants and could explode any minute; this is true of some countries in the region, yet all remain worried about the threat of terrorism. Parts of the region, in any case, represent more of a precarious situation than others. Countries such as Uzbekistan, Tajikistan, and Kyrgyzstan have real problems with Islamist groups. Some of these groups have close ties to al-Qaida, such as the East Turkestan Islamic Movement.

Olcott states in her testimony that "there is convincing evidence that Uzbek security forces needed to use considerable force to break up a terrorist training camp in the mountainous border regions of southeast Uzbekistan (in an area that abuts both Afghanistan and Tajikistan). There was also strong evidence linking the IMU for armed incursions on the territory of the Kyrgyz republic, in 1999."[2] Furthermore, there is convincing evidence that the Islamic Movement of Uzbekistan had clear relations with al-Qaida.

It comes as no surprise that a Sunni Islamist group would have a relationship with al-Qaida. In fact this is what al-Qaida is all about. This is what Osama bin Laden established when he set out to launch his pan-Islamist movement; his strength, so to speak, lies in his Rolodex.

Al-Qaida means "the base" in Arabic, but it could also mean "the (data) base." Bin Laden is reported by journalists who have met him to have kept meticulous files of the fighters he recruited, along with all their vital statistics.

One of his strengths was precisely his vast network. Al-Qaida is said to have an amazing operation spread across more than sixty countries, though but I really don't believe bin Laden had personal envoys, al-Qaida men on his payroll scattered all over the world.

Do you realize the logistics needed for such an organization? It would mean regular bank transfers that eventually could be traced. It would require regular communications between the base and the people in the field. It would require a support group at the base of operations practically as sophisticated as the intelligence service of a middle-sized country. One doesn't run such a network on half a dozen pay-as-you-go cell phones from a cave in the Afghan mountains. One would need serious communication equipment and enough power to keep all that hardware going around the clock. If all this was hooked up to a public electric grid, it should show up on the electric company's counters. If bin Laden is generating his own electricity, then the heat signature from his generators should be visible from space and easily picked up by satellites.

And finally, one doesn't have a network as vast as what he is reported to have had and not risk a serious leak. Rather, what I believe bin Laden does have is a great list of contacts and possible working arrangements with various Islamist organizations that sympathize with his cause.

The Center for Defense Information (CDI), a Washington, D.C.–based independent group, lists Kazakhstan at number 30, the last place on their list, along with the United States, as countries on the receiving end of terrorism operations.

Given Kazakhstan's interest in terrorism prevention, what the country is doing is quite impressive. In fact, what the Kazakhs are doing is called pre-emption. The government in Astana is trying to do what no other country has done in the past: address the issue of terrorism from both ends simultaneously.

Indeed, it is also called understanding what is needed to fight terrorism and contain it. In fact, professionals in the field of conflict resolution rarely talk about doing away with a conflict altogether. Instead they talk about containing a conflict.

As much of today's terrorism emanates largely from religious groups, involving religion in finding the solution to the problem is perhaps the key to solving this problem that in the past decade has continued to feed upon itself.

Terrorism can only be defeated by a two-pronged approach. The first approach is through the use of traditional brute military force and aggressive intelligence gathering, from both human intelligence and the use of electronic data gathering. In other words, track them, study them, and eliminate them as a threat, to the extent that it is possible. But this approach alone has produced limited results. We have ample proof from two major conflicts—Palestine and Afghanistan—that military force alone is insufficient to solve the issue, as is the best intelligence money can buy. It will only buy some time.

After six decades of the Israel-Palestine conflict and almost ten years of trying that approach in Afghanistan, the results are dismal. The Taliban are hardly worse off today than they were eight years ago (other than the loss of Kabul), and that is after taking on the world's mightiest army and its allies. And the Palestinian issue keeps morphing into a more dangerous form, implicating new actors every year. Can we continue to refer to it as the "Arab-Israeli dispute," when the conflict has evolved beyond the Arab world with Turkey and Iran now involved in one manner or another?

So if military might is not the solution to eradicating terrorism, then what is the answer? The solution, or at least part of it, is to be found in the second approach, in exactly what Kazakhstan is doing today. It is a more humanitarian approach to address the issue from the opposite end, meaning to tackle the social and economic aspect of the problem (as discussed in the previous chapter in greater detail) by involving those who seem to matter the most in these conflicts—the leaders of the religious establishments. Otherwise, the military option on its own is destined to fail.

The second approach calls for showing the developing world that the more prosperous parts of the globe do care for them. Here is how it should work, using the Afghan conflict as an example. The outcome of the war in Afghanistan concerns the Kazakhs directly, and the violence and terrorism tearing Afghanistan apart is based on religion.

All throughout history, Afghan fighters have faced armies that were far superior in numbers to the forces they could muster to defend their territory, and they have faced armies with far superior training and armament.

In more recent history, the Afghans faced the British when Great Britain was truly a great power, and they fought off the Soviet invasion. Though the Soviets did occupy the country, they never really dominated it. The Afghans have always been able to set an ambush and then vanish into the rugged mountains, where modern armies find it impossible to follow.

The Soviets, who were the second superpower in the world at the time, and reputed to have one of the best intelligence networks in Central Asia, faced a real challenge when it came to fighting the Afghan resistance. They tried bombing the Afghan resistance out of existence. They tried assassinations of Afghan leaders. They tried and tried and tried, and in the end they had to give up and return home in defeat.

After trying to eliminate the Afghan leadership, the Soviets, and now the Americans, failed to realize that every time one was killed there were multiple others ready to take his place. That is true of most conflicts, be they in Central Asia, the Middle East, or elsewhere. The result of such a policy is that it only aggravated the situation, much as the conflict in the Middle East that began initially as a dispute over real estate has now turned into a religious war, rendering the problem that much more difficult and complex because God is involved.

With this approach, the first enemy that is created is right there in Afghanistan, among the relatives of the victim. The next enemy they create will typically be a young Muslim in some place such as Pakistan, India, Tajikistan, Uzbekistan, or Indonesia. Eventually, one of those young people, very probably a graduate of one of the religious schools, will be moved to join a radical movement. Again, the same holds true for Iraq and Palestine.

The answer lies in giving people reasons to live and let live, rather than reasons to die and to want to kill. This is why the Kazakh leadership is working hard to promote dialogue, tolerance, and understanding among religious leaders, hoping that message will sink in and eventually trickle down.

The question of Palestine has been at the center of many of the Islamists' complaints. Bin Laden stated that he was fighting in part to seek revenge for what the Israelis had done to the Palestinians. Whether that is true or is simply an excuse to gather the troops around him, it is nevertheless a good explanation. All the reason more to solve the Arab-Israeli-Iranian-Turkish conflict before it grows and more names are added to that list.

There may have never been a terrorist attack on Kazakh soil, but that does not mean the authorities are sleeping on the job, or that they are not worried that it may happen. Far from it. The security services in Kazakhstan are discreet; they are very different from their former employers in Soviet Russia. Nevertheless, they are vigilant and are on constant watch. They have no other options, given the neighborhood they live in where *Salafi* and *Takfiri* groups are active. Kazakhstan is a quiet country, but all around there is much potential for trouble.

How and why did the Islamist issue become an issue? For the vast majority of Americans, the "war on terror," as President George W. Bush used to
call it, began with the 9/11 attacks. For them, the anti-terror campaign can
be filed neatly into two folders: before and after September 11, 2001. The
truth of the matter is that the war on *terrorism*[3] has been going on for the
better part of eight decades, if not longer. Here is an example that the war on
terrorism is not that new: the cover of the October 31, 1977, issue of *Time*
magazine reads, "War on Terrorism." That was twenty-four years before the
9/11 attacks. It's just that nobody in the United States seemed to take notice
until it hit home.

The fact is that terrorism has evolved over the years, changing its face and
changing its targets. Thankfully, Kazakhstan has been spared from terrorism,
be it Islamist terrorism or any other. The reasons are many, but partially it is
owing to pure luck and certainly to the sharpness of the country's security
services. The other reason, perhaps, is that the Kazakhs have not really drawn
the ire of anyone to the point of attracting terrorism, not that this argument
holds water with the people who are responsible for placing bombs and sending young men (and at times women, too) to become "martyrs."

What is it in fact that motivates someone to pack explosives on themselves
and go kill total strangers? What is it that pushed nineteen men to hijack airplanes and fly them into buildings? Once again we need to turn back the pages
of history in order to understand how and why these groups turned to terrorism as a political tool, and how we reached the point we are at today.

The story of today's Islamoterrorism is a complicated and controversial
one, with people of different opinions placing the blame on different parties.
Additionally, the very question of who is a terrorist remains unsettled, and the
United Nations is not even trying to get anywhere near that issue. It would
raise a ruckus in the General Assembly when countries tried to get other countries classified as "terrorists" and delegations stormed out in protest. Rightfully so, the UN has opted to remain clear of that thorny topic.

Indeed sensitivities are such that even an honest attempt at explaining
certain situations can be taken out of context. I was once invited by my alma
mater, Royal Roads University, to give a lecture on the Lebanese civil war. I
decided that rather than using the generally accepted date of April 13, 1975,
as the starting date of the conflict, I would look deeper into the causes that

allowed the conflict to take place. I therefore looked for a key event in history to use as a starting point.

In short, I had reached the following conclusion: The civil war would not have happened had the Palestinian resistance not relocated to Lebanon from Jordan in 1970. In turn, the PLO would not have existed if Palestinians were not forced to flee the conflicts of 1948 (the creation of the State of Israel) and June 1967 (the Six-Day War). Taking it even further back, these wars would not have happened had Theodor Herzl not declared the need for a Jewish homeland at the first Zionist Congress in Basle, Switzerland, in 1897. I was not laying blame on any party but trying to put historical facts in evidence. Still, my analysis upset an Israeli student.

In a similar fashion, the analysis outlined below tracing the roots of Islamist terrorism is my personal view of how a number of events unfolded leading to the current dilemma. I have drawn on my personal experience as a journalist covering the crisis for more than thirty years.

The root of today's Islamist terrorism can be traced to three different sources: the first has its roots in Egypt with the Muslim Brotherhood[4] (MB), the second has its origins in the Israeli-Palestinian conflict, and the third came to be as a result of the Soviet invasion of Afghanistan in 1979. These are three separate historic events that at first may seem unrelated and perhaps even somewhat confusing to a reader unfamiliar with the contemporary history of the region, but they end up converging and giving us the bigger picture. The three roads eventually end up merging into a single lane.

The first road is that of the *Ikhwan*, or Brotherhood, which was founded in Egypt in 1926 by a schoolteacher called Hassan al-Banna. The aim of the organization is to have Muslim countries accept the Quran and the *Sunnah*[5] as the sole reference point for Muslims around the world. Officially the movement opposes violence, with exception to the Israeli-Palestinian conflict. The MB also turned to violence in its battle with the Syrian government, a secular regime that has banned the MB and hunted down and arrested its members in Syria.[6]

The Brotherhood's resorting to violence as a means of achieving their political goals has long been in question, as the Egyptian government accused the MB of a series of assassinations and consequently banned the movement. Belonging to the Muslim Brotherhood is forbidden in Egypt and its members are regularly jailed. It is in jail where most members of the MB turn to violence, usually after undergoing torture at the hands of their jailers. It was in jail that Dr. Ayman al-Zawahiri, al-Qaida's number-two man, turned radical and decided to join Osama bin Laden's group.

The Brotherhood overcomes the ban on its members from running for office by having them run as independents. Officially the group denounces terrorism and they have condemned the September 11, 2001, attacks. Still, their direct links to terrorism remain questionable. The issue of whether or not to resort to violence has led to schisms within the MB and the formation of breakaway groups such as Al-Gama'a al-Islamiyya[7] and Takfir wal-Hijra.[8] One of the most prominent members of the MB was the writer Sayyid Qutb.[9]

The Brotherhood is active in nearly every country in the world, including in parts of Central Asia and the United States. Naturally, they often go by different names in different countries, as the ban on the MB goes beyond the borders of Egypt. Although the Brotherhood is banned in Egypt, it remains the strongest and most popular political party and it would win elections today, if free elections were held. Many observers, however, believe that if the Brotherhood did win elections they might very well be the last elections, as the Brotherhood subscribes to the "one man, one vote, one time" philosophy.

The story of the Brotherhood since its founding has been pretty much consistent with their ultimate aim of Muslim countries adopting sharia law, and one of their main concerns is fighting corruption, an issue that has won them much support among the working class. There are those in the West who argue that the Brotherhood's ultimate aim is to spread Islam to the entire world. Initially concerned with the political situation in Egypt, the movement eventually became pan-Arab and now has global representation. The MB gets its funding from donations from its members.

The second source of terrorism in the Middle East began as Arab terrorists and Jewish terrorists fought over land issues in Palestine during the British Mandate, and it was for the most part restricted to the territory of Palestine, as both Jews and Arabs carried out attacks against each other and against the British. Former Israeli prime minister Menachem Begin was on the British terrorist list for being a member of the outlawed Irgun, and for his participation in blowing up the King David Hotel in Jerusalem.

Arab terrorism against Western interests, however, began in earnest in the aftermath of the June 1967 Six-Day War, a crushing and humiliating defeat for the Arabs. In just six days the Israeli army, then less than two decades in existence, launched preemptive strikes against three of its neighbors and occupied the entire Sinai Peninsula and the Gaza Strip from Egypt, the Golan Heights from Syria, and East Jerusalem and the West Bank of the Jordan River from Jordan.

In is likely that the Six-Day War represents the biggest loss of territory, prestige, and honor for the Arabs since the defeat of 1948, when Israel declared its independence and repulsed attacks by the Arab armies on multiple fronts, which followed the creation of the Jewish State. It was obvious that before any peace negotiations could begin, the Arabs had to recapture some of that lost honor.

The Arab defeat of 1967 led to two major developments in the Middle East and beyond. First, it led to the planning of the next war, the October 1973 War, also known in Israel as the Yom Kippur War. The war marks an important turning point in the Arab-Israeli conflict for two reasons: One, it made the Israelis realize that they were not as undefeatable as the 1967 war led them to believe. Two, it gave the Arabs back some of the lost honor from the Six-Day War and allowed them to sit at the negotiating table with the Israelis. This led to the Camp David Peace Accords and took Egypt out of the conflict. It also led to the assassination of Egyptian president Anwar Sadat by a man with links to the Muslim Brotherhood.

The second effect of 1967 was that it awoke Palestinian national sentiments and led them to take their fate into their own hands. It was at this point that a civil engineer originally from Gaza by the name of Yasser Arafat took over the leadership of the Palestine Liberation Organization (PLO), which until this point was under Egyptian tutelage. Arafat and his PLO based themselves in the Jordanian capital, Amman, and began launching commando operations against Israel. Israel retaliated against Jordan, leading to much tension between the Palestinians and the Jordanians.

All this reached a crux when an attempt was made on the life of King Hussein of Jordan in September 1970. Heavy fighting erupted between the Palestinian commandos and the Jordanian army and quickly spread from the capital to engulf the entire country. The month-long confrontation became known as Black September and resulted in the expulsion of the PLO and other Palestinian armed groups from Jordan. The PLO and its affiliates relocated to Lebanon, where before long the same mistakes were committed.

Continued raids by Palestinian fighters across the Lebanese frontier led to retaliatory raids by Israel on Lebanese territory, and much of the brunt of these attacks was directed at areas inhabited by Lebanese Shiite Muslims and also led to frequent clashes between the Shiites and the Palestinians.

In the years between the arrival of the PLO in Lebanon in 1970 and their expulsion by Israel in 1982, Lebanon went through a long civil war that gave the Palestinian resistance a free hand in the areas under their control. It was during this time that some of the PLO groups, such as the Popular Front for the Liberation of Palestine and the Democratic Front for the Liberation of Palestine, began to make contact with international terrorist organizations, such as the Japanese Red Army, Italy's Red Brigades, the West German Baader-Meinhoff Gang, and others. Airline hijacking had become a favorite method of the Palestinian groups.

Eventually, when Israel invaded Lebanon in June 1982 after an attempt by a Palestinian terrorist group to assassinate Shlomo Argov, the Israeli ambassador in London, the Shiite population in the south Lebanese villages and towns greeted the Israelis as liberators.

But before long the Israelis had overstayed their welcome and soon relations with the Shiites began to sour. The Shiites began to get organized and soon Hezbollah, the Party of God, was formed (with Iranian assistance). The relevance of this second link—the Palestinian-Hezbollah link—may appear unrelated to today's struggle undertaken by Islamic terrorist groups, as the Palestinians in recent years have directed their war against Israel. Hamas, the Palestinian Islamic Resistance Movement, though on the U.S. terrorist list, has also restricted its actions against Israel, but there is still the Iran connection to keep in mind.

The third source of Islamist terrorism, and probably the one with the most relevance and ties to today's Islamist terrorists and the closest in terms of threat level to the countries of Central Asia, came about as a result of the Soviet invasion of Afghanistan in 1979 and the subsequent assistance supplied by the United States to mujahideen. The thinking at the time was that supporting Islamist groups in their fight against the godless Communists was a good idea.

This is where Osama bin Laden and his al-Qaida organization enter the scene. A Saudi national of Yemeni origin, bin Laden made his fortune in the construction business in Saudi Arabia. He arrived in Afghanistan with his group of "Afghan-Arabs," as they became known, a sort of Islamic version of the Lincoln Brigade[10] because they were Arabs, many from Saudi Arabia and Yemen, who volunteered to fight in Afghanistan in the name of Islam to help defeat the Soviets. At that point the mujahideen were considered to be the "good guys" fighting on the side of the United States.

At the end of the war, believing that the struggle was over, the United States packed up and left Afghanistan, stranding thousands of these Afghan-Arabs. They began to slowly disperse, some going on to fight in Bosnia and Chechnya. Others made their way to Saudi Arabia and Yemen, where they joined up with local networks of jihadis, and many stayed in contact with bin Laden and his al-Qaida operation.

We now need to fast forward to the Iraqi invasion of Kuwait in August 1990 when Saddam Hussein ordered his troops to cross the border and take over the tiny oil-rich emirate. Kuwait's 20,000-strong armed forces, who had never been in combat, were no match for the 1 million–strong Iraqi army with eight years of combat experience from the war with Iran. Iraqi troops were now within easy reach of Saudi Arabia and the world's largest oil fields.

Saddam hesitated about whether to continue into Saudi Arabia or stop. In fact the Iraqi dictator committed three very grave mistakes in occupying Kuwait, which he called Iraq's nineteenth province. The invasion was sparked by a long-standing dispute between the two countries over oil fields being exploited by Kuwait that were in an area called the Neutral Zone that straddled the border between the two countries. Saddam claimed the Kuwaitis were drilling perpendicularly, tapping into Iraqi oil.

Iraq was hurting financially from the war with Iran and had hoped to raise the price on a barrel of oil, a move Kuwait opposed. But had the Iraqis taken the oil wells in the Neutral Zone and stopped, chances are nothing more would have happened.

If Saddam had ordered his forces to continue all the way into Saudi Arabia and occupy the entire Arabian Peninsula, it is questionable whether the United States would have committed itself to liberating all of Saudi Arabia, given the losses it would have involved. As it turns out, Saddam hesitated after taking Kuwait, and this gave the United States the time it needed to dispatch a group of U.S. Marines to Saudi Arabia.

The U.S. Marine Expeditionary Unit (MEU) that arrived within a couple of days in the Saudi port of Dhahran would have not been able to stop an eventual Iraqi attack on their own, but their presence there was enough to deter the Iraqis from crossing the border and allow for a massive buildup of coalition forces that began in August 1990 and continued until February 1991.

Osama bin Laden was irritated by the presence of U.S. and other foreign soldiers as they began to arrive on Saudi territory, the land of the two holy mosques of Mecca and Medina, and requested an audience with the king. According to an eyewitness account from someone who was in the room at the time, apparently bin Laden asked the king to have the Americans leave so that he and his Afghan Arabs could get the Iraqis out of Kuwait.

The report from that meeting states that the king laughed at the proposal, telling bin Laden that the Iraqi army was the strongest Arab army and that they could not possibly be beaten by his ragtag group. Bin Laden stormed out and it seems that it was at that point that he made up his mind that the monarchy in Saudi Arabia was as bad as the Americans, and that his war now included getting rid of the monarchy in Saudi Arabia. Thus began his campaign against the West and moderate Arabs.

Thousands of people have lost their lives to religion-based terrorism around the world in the last few years. Most, if not all, of them were innocent. They just happened to be at the wrong place at the wrong time. Not to underestimate the threat of *Takfiri* terrorism, but it would be terribly wrong to assume that Muslims are the only terrorists worth watching out for today. Yet there are a growing number of Americans who believe that *all* Muslims in the United States represent a potential danger to the country's national security.

As a recent CNN special investigation,[11] based on a study by researchers at the University of North Carolina at Chapel Hill, pointed out, the "terrorist threat posed by radicalized Muslim-Americans has been exaggerated." The report states that the number of Muslim Americans who have crossed over the line to join up with terrorist groups is seventeen per year. The report calls this a small number. Indeed, seventeen people joining the ranks of those who swore to fight the United States is nothing worth writing home about. But, wait a minute. How many were involved in the 9/11 attacks? Nineteen, right?

Furthermore, the report has a major flaw in that the numbers mentioned— 17 per year, or the 139 individuals categorized as "Muslim-American terrorism offenders"—had to have had prior history with law authorities. To make the list one had to have "been wanted, arrested, convicted or killed in connection with terrorism-related activities since 9/11—and have lived in the United States, regardless of immigration status, for more than a year prior to arrest."

It has been generally admitted that since the 9/11 attacks there has been increased tension among Muslim Americans about their acceptance in mainstream American society, as the study shows. Muslim Americans report feeling a stronger anti-Muslim bias from the media, as well as from day-to-day interactions. Overall, Muslim Americans understand and support the need for enhanced security and counterterrorism initiatives, but the report finds that some believe these efforts are discriminatory. "Governments can promote and encourage the building of strong Muslim American communities and promote outreach by social services agencies," reported CNN. Perhaps they, too, should come to Kazakhstan.

―――――――

The calm that prevails in Kazakhstan has not deterred the authorities here from worrying about religious extremism percolating all around them. The Kazakhs take their security concerns very seriously. As Kanat Saudabayev, the country's foreign minister and secretary of state, indicated at a conference last year organized by the OSCE and grouping a number of experts in the field of counterterrorism, Kazakhstan is not concerned by terrorists but by the threats of terrorism. "We live in a dangerous geopolitical place," said Ardak Doszhan, chairman of the Committee on Religious Affairs at the Ministry of Culture. He explained that Kazakhstan was sitting in the center of a very tumultuous region, where a number of soft insurgencies were brewing and could erupt any minute.

Among the most visible in Kazakhstan's immediate neighborhood are the Uyghur, the Chinese Muslims, whose sometimes troubled province of Xinjiang borders Kazakhstan's eastern frontier. There are periodic bouts of trouble in China's predominantly Muslim province, though of course Beijing likes to keep things under wrap. The Uyghur are far from being united, something that plays in favor of Beijing for the moment.

Some Uyghur have a pan-Islamic vision, and look to the East Turkestan Islamic Movement as an example to follow; others lean more toward some sort of a pan-Turkic vision, as in the East Turkestan Liberation Organization; and still others support the vision of an independent "Uyghurstan," as does the East Turkestan Independence movement. Some Uyghur who believe that other Uyghur are too deeply assimilated in Russian and Chinese culture have resorted to acts of violence. All of these are developments the Kazakhs are keeping a close eye on.

On the other side of the country, on Kazakhstan's western border, sits Dagestan, another troubled spot worth keeping a watchful eye on, especially given that it is on Russian territory and comes with its own set of liberation movements.

To the southwest is Uzbekistan, a hotbed of Islamist activity. Periodically droves of Uzbek political and/or economic refugees make their way across the border seeking shelter or employment in Kazakhstan. The authorities in Astana know very well that with every new wave of refugees are a number of Islamist militants seeking to recruit young Kazakhs to their cause.

No doubt that some make it past the Kazakh security dragnet, but many do not. Ardak Doszhan from the Ministry of Culture comments that the country's security forces are "very effective." To the southeast Kazakhstan borders Kyrgyzstan, another source of continuous domestic problems. These concern the Kazakh authorities because of the fear that some Islamist thoughts could eventually trickle down into Kazakh society.

Despite much criticism from the West, and particularly from human rights groups, that Kazakhstan is dragging its heels in establishing democracy as perceived by the West, Kazakhstan is today a shining example in Central Asia where the other "stans" have still a long way to go before they achieve the level of political maturity seen in Kazakhstan.

Finally, to conclude this chapter on terrorism, here is a quick puzzle: What do Islamist fundamentalists and Central Asian drug and prostitution cartels have in common? Indeed, what could Islamist radicals, who will not hesitate to resort to terrorism, have in common with regional drug lords and criminal gangs running prostitution rings in the former Soviet republics? What are the chances of those strange bedfellows actually working toward the same goal, that of destabilizing the Central Asian republic of Kyrgyzstan?

After the political chaos in Kyrgyzstan, which came about following the April 2010 coup, there is reason to believe that there has been close cooperation between drug cartels and Islamist fundamentalists. Cooperation between Islamist fundamentalists and drug lords has already been established with proof of various Latin American drug barons selling their goods to Islamist groups operating throughout Africa, who then resell their illicit cargo on European markets.

The first question one needs to ask is why would these diametrically opposed groups with very different agendas and entirely different philosophies choose to continue to destabilize a country and to finance and arm the ousted president and his followers to the point that it may contribute to igniting a full-scale civil war in Kyrgyzstan? Yet a senior high-ranking diplomat based in Astana indicated that such forces are at work trying hard to destabilize Kyrgyzstan.

The diplomat, who asked not to be identified, pointed out the fact that the drug cartels, the Islamists, and the people running the modern slave trade—that is the dismal conditions under which young women are lured into prostitution throughout Central Asia—would all profit tremendously in the event of civil war in the Central Asian republic.

These are yet more reasons for Kazakhstan to remain vigilant and to push for a peaceful resolution of the different conflicts. From this perspective, Kazakhstan has a vested interest in keeping the region peaceful.

ELEVEN

Kazakhstan's Role in Shaping Central Asia

"Do not follow where the path may lead. Go instead where there is no path and leave a trail."

—*Harold R. McAlindon, author and management expert*

T he government in Kazakhstan is taking its efforts to promote inter-faith understanding and to prevent the threats of terrorism to heart. What is very different in the Kazakh approach when dealing with the issue of terrorism is the notion of "preventing the threat of terrorism," rather than simply "preventing terrorism."

Though the distinction may not sound like much, there is nevertheless a world of difference between the two approaches to dealing with one of the most serious questions affecting our world today. When we talk about preventing terrorism it generally means that there is already a situation where acts of terrorism are a distinct possibility, as is the current situation in the United States, for example.

Since the 9/11 attacks the country has been on alert trying to prevent further acts of terrorism from being carried out in the United States or against American interests overseas. Overall, one could say the U.S. government has been largely successful in preventing terrorism on its home soil, as well as against American interests abroad.

On the other hand, the United States has a dismal record at preventing the threat of terrorism. The reason for that requires some analysis. Because the United States has been so caught up in fighting terrorism and preventing terrorism, little or no attention has been given to fighting the "threat of terrorism," something that requires a far more intricate undertaking than does fighting terrorism. Stay with me for a moment as we analyze the differences. They are important to the overall strategy of the ongoing war on terrorism.

Preventing terrorism means deploying military and/or security and intelligence personnel to counter an imminent threat of a potential terrorist attack. Most countries in the world today are at risk of terrorism, thus they are engaged in preventing terrorism. Those include traditional security measures against possible terrorism actions, such as routine airport checks, intelligence gathering, and the usual covert action that the regular citizen rarely gets an opportunity to see.

On the intelligence side of things, it means having to infiltrate the terrorist networks through human intelligence, which is difficult and dangerous for the agents in the field, or through electronic intelligence-gathering systems such as satellite technology, but that is not always perfect as the terrorists have learned how to outsmart the smart technology.

When countries reach the stage of terrorism prevention it usually means that there are no longer any lines of communication between the two sides, that all lines or almost all lines of communications are down, as occurs at times in the Israeli-Palestinian conflict; or that no lines of communications were established in the first place, as with al-Qaida.

Preventing the threat of terrorism, on the other hand, means as a first step identifying what are the root problems of what is driving the terrorists to take up arms and to resort to violence as a means of political expression. It means identifying what concrete actions can be implemented. It then requires firm follow-up actions to address the issues at hand, assuming they can be addressed.

It also means accepting the reality that when dealing with terrorism there are basically two sorts of terrorists: negotiable terrorists and non-negotiable terrorists.

The negotiable terrorists are usually groups who are fighting for a national cause (Hamas in the Palestinian Territories). Their actions are usually delimited to the geographic location of the country in question, or they may be based in one country and operate in another for logistics reasons. Example: The

Kurds based in Iraqi Kurdistan might cross the border into Turkey and launch attacks against the Turkish military, then retreat back across the border in Iraq.

The non-negotiable terrorists are those with whom any attempt at reaching a workable peace accord is just impossible because their charter calls for continued struggle or there is absolutely no hope of ever establishing a middle ground and a basis for negotiations: for example, al-Qaida.

When dealing with the threat of terrorism it means trying to understand what it is that motivates this particular terrorist movement and then addressing its root problems. This means dealing with the problem from a social, economic, and political level. This approach is preferable to waiting for the problem to develop to the point where those who resort to violence to have their voices heard begin carrying out terrorist attacks.

In order to achieve this, economies that are broken need to be repaired so that jobs can be created and given to those who need them. With a job and steady income men and women in the poorer strata of society will not be so eager to join up with religious fanatics, for the most part.

It means for the developed world to prop up governments in need of assistance so that they in turn provide better services to their citizens, as is expected from governments. It is no coincidence that the countries with weak governments or failed states are the ones where terrorist movements are typically very active.

With that in mind it is now easier to understand what motivates a country such as Kazakhstan to become so involved in addressing the issue of the threat of terrorism.

Hardly a week goes by in Astana without a high-level meeting of some sort taking place that has to deal with either the topic of international terrorism or interreligious tolerance and understanding. I exaggerate, of course, but there seems to be a season when the conventions seem to be taking place back-to-back.

Walk around one of the super-modern convention centers that stand out in a futuristic-looking segment of the city, such as the Palace of Independence or the Pyramid, a large glass pyramid housing, among others, a convention center and the Ministry of Culture, and you are more likely than not to run into some famous people. This is what is referred to in Astana as "the new city."

During one week I met actor Armand Assante, who was in Kazakhstan shooting a documentary for PBS. He ended up interviewing me, rather than the other way around. But that is not unusual in Astana, where the unexpected happens. I mean this in a nice sort of way; you never know whom you will run into. Other famous people that are said to visit often and unrelated to the conferences are Elton John and King Abdullah of Jordan. Several members of the British royal family are said to visit periodically, as well. But it's all kept very low key, except for Elton John, of course, whose posters are seen all over the city announcing his next show.

Kazakhstan remains somewhat of a secret vacation spot for the more adventurous of the rich and famous. Maybe it's because this is one of the few places left in the world where nature is still preserved, or because it's one of the few places in the world that paparazzi have not yet discovered and can serve as a last refuge where the actions of these celebrities will not be splashed across the front pages of the tabloid press.

I also saw Imam Feisal Abdul Rauf, the Muslim cleric at the center of the Ground Zero controversy. Thinking that he was acting in good faith and believing that his idea would contribute to his lifelong labor of trying to bridge the gap between Islam and the Judeo-Christian world, the imam who runs the Cordoba Initiative had suggested building a mosque at the site of the World Trade Center. Only his idea backfired and he found himself on the receiving end of insults and death threats. The imam is an old acquaintance whom I met prior to this mess he found himself in. We walked together through the convention center for a few minutes before he had to go back to participate in the debates. Since the controversy over the Ground Zero mosque suggestion back in the United States, the imam cannot go anywhere without federal police protection.

Of course there are clerics from all faiths wandering around in their different colored robes. From Iranian clerics, representing the Islamic Republic, who always appear stern and far too serious, to Sufi followers who project an aura of friendship and serenity, to Buddhist monks in their saffron robes and with walking sticks, to other representatives of the "traditional faiths": imams, priests, pastors, and rabbis. They are all here.

Some of these meetings take on more importance than others, depending on the level of invitees; in any case most of these conferences are held under the patronage of President Nazarbayev or Foreign Minister Saudabayev and attract the top names of prominent people in their respective fields.

Terrorism and religion are topics that preoccupy the Kazakh government a great deal and with good reason. Terrorism and religion have been the drivers of recent geopolitics in Central Asia ever since the breakup of the Soviet Union. Indeed, terrorism and religion have been driving politics in other parts of the world, as well, from Europe to the Middle East and beyond.

Since September 11, 2001, the terrorism in question has been largely motivated by religion. Or at least those who perpetrate these terrorist acts presume to represent a religious movement and more often than not they purport to be acting and speaking on behalf of God. All the religious and political leaders that have come to Astana will tell anyone willing to listen than no God that they know of condones terrorism. Regardless of what you choose to call this god, there is no god who will accept that innocents die in his name.

What is particularly interesting about Kazakhstan's involvement in dealing with both terrorism and religion is the level of commitment from a country that has never directly suffered from terrorism, nor for that matter is it overly religious. Even the chief mufti pointed out to me that Kazakhstan is a secular country where religion plays a very small role in the daily lives of the average person.

Regretfully though, not enough is known about Kazakhstan's efforts to bridge the two sides and to launch a dialogue between the Muslim East and Christian West. Indeed, very little is known about this country in the West, where great misconceptions about the country, its culture, its modernity, and its achievements dominate among the population at large. Few people in the United States would be able to situate it on a map, and a number of times when I called my bank or credit card service and told them I was calling from Kazakhstan, the reply was, "I will not even attempt to spell that."

Yet, Kazakhstan is the ninth-largest country in the world. That makes it larger than France, England, Germany, Mexico, and more that one hundred other countries. At the time of the breakup of the Soviet Union it was the fourth largest nuclear power, a position of prestige it voluntarily gave up. Consider this for a moment the next time you may have the urge to depict all Muslims as having the same agenda.

When I mention to people back in the United States that I had spent the first six months of 2010 living in Kazakhstan, their immediate reaction is usually one of disbelief. First, one has to explain where Kazakhstan is located. Then one has to answer questions such as, "Why would you want to go there?" The next inane statement is something such as, "That must have been terrible."

They imagine an Afghanistan-like country, ripped apart by internal strife and littered with Islamist terrorists. Nothing could be further from the truth. More regretfully, the only news stories from Kazakhstan that seem to interest Western newspaper editors are stories that more often than not depict Kazakhstan negatively. As they say, good news is not worth reporting and therefore reports of progress and strides toward democracy are sidelined in favor of stories about human rights abuses. As a colleague once said, "You will never see a headline saying 'Plane lands safely.'"

On the question of human rights abuses: Did they take place? Of course they did. But then again so have there been human rights abuses carried out by U.S. military and civilian personnel in detention facilities such as Guantánamo Bay and the Abu Ghraib prison in Baghdad. Granted, two wrongs do not make one right, but the fact remains that Kazakhstan has made great strides and deserves to be recognized for that.

On a somewhat more optimistic note, it is worth mentioning that all is not gloom and doom and that the future does look brighter. There exists a viable solution to the problem causing so much pain to the international community, as well as to the majority of Muslims, but that solution must come from within the Muslim community. The solution, or at least part of the solution, is *Ijtihad*. If the gates of *Ijtihad* were to reopen, the outcome could be as monumental for Islam as Vatican II was for Catholicism.

The Second Ecumenical Council of the Vatican, also known as Vatican II, was the Catholic Church's twenty-first ecumenical council. It lasted nearly three years, opening on October 11, 1962, and concluding its work on December 8, 1965. Throughout the 1950s, theological and biblical studies of the Catholic Church had begun to deviate from the neo-scholasticism and biblical literalism that the reaction to modernism had enforced since Vatican I. Reformers wanted to integrate modern human experience with Christian dogma. The last such council, Vatican I, had been held nearly a century earlier, but the proceedings were interrupted when the Italian army marched into Rome to unify the country.

At that time the Catholic Church faced political, social, and economic challenges owing to changes brought about by an evolving society. In a certain way the problems facing the Catholic Church were not very different from those currently facing Islam, with two major exceptions. First, the Catholic Church was losing followers, whereas Islam is the fastest-growing religion in the world today. This of course could be an incentive to maintain the status quo. But what plays in favor of advocating for change is the violent streak that is affecting Islam today. The violence emanating from Islamist terrorists has claimed thousands of lives and left practically no country untouched, including many Muslim nations. That should be enough incentive to enact change and should be done sooner rather than later.

Another major difference between Sunni Islam and Catholicism, in terms of structure, is that unlike the Catholic Church, there is no central figure in Islam like the pope, nor is there a central seat of authority such as the Vatican. In the Sunni branch of Islam, every cleric has equal standing.

Agreeing over the correct time to break the fast at the end of the holy month of Ramadan is just one prime example of the confusion that may arise. Traditionally, Muslims who observe the fast are permitted to break their fast at sunset. However, arguments have broken out over which location should be the "official" place where the new moon first appears, signaling the end of Ramadan: Casablanca in Morocco at the far west end of the Arab world, or Mecca in Saudi Arabia on the eastern end of the Arab world. Geographically speaking there is a difference of about three hours between the two cities— much more if you factor in the Muslims in Central Asia. Such is the freedom or autonomy enjoyed by individual imams.

At the same time, this autonomy allows for confusion to some degree. One negative example is that any imam, no matter how educated in sharia or in the Quran, is allowed to issue religious edicts, or fatwas. There is something to be said for centralizing authority as France, Turkey, and Kazakhstan have done.

From the time the gates of *Ijtihad* were closed, scholars and jurists were to rely only on the original meaning and earlier interpretations of the Quran and the Hadith. Today that remains the fundamental question that many scholars of Islam are debating. Two primary questions jump to mind. Just how much change should be implemented, and who should be authorized to make those changes? Those are genuine concerns, and if those two questions were ever addressed, then reopening the gates of *Ijtihad* would be one step closer to reality.

There is some good news in all of this. The movement among scholars and intellectuals to revive the practice of *Ijtihad* seems to be growing and slowly gathering momentum. Today, Muslim society is experiencing turbulence; the intra-Muslim differences of opinion, the wars in Iraq and Afghanistan, the continued occupation of Palestinian lands, the frustrations caused by oppressive regimes, and the absence of democracy have all conspired to give birth to a radical, politicized, and violent form of Islam whose adherents have turned to terror as a means of achieving their aims. They have indeed politicized and radicalized Islam, and it must be de-politicized and de-radicalized.

The reward for such a policy of preventing the threat of terrorism will pay dividends tenfold. That is why investing in preventing the threat of terrorism, in other words addressing the problem before it becomes one, is smart policy. This is not an easy approach and it requires resources, commitment, and perseverance. In the long run it will pay off. Not only will it stop the spread of terrorism, but it will also create better environments in societies at home.

TWELVE

Can Democracy and Islam Coexist?

"Democracy does not guarantee equality of conditions—it only guarantees equality of opportunity."

—*John Dryden, poet*

Peaceful policies in Kazakhstan is the basis of our politics," said Yeraly Tugzhanov, vice chairman of the Kazakhstan Assembly during a discussion in his office in the imposing Government Building.[1] The tall and modern edifice is one of several such buildings situated in a very large and vast plaza the size of probably half a dozen football fields.

This is one of the newer neighborhoods of the capital, where everything is clean and shiny and in winter kept ice-free by a small army of municipal workers who work practically around the clock. This is an area populated mostly by government offices. The buildings stand on either side of the imposing presidential palace, the Akorda, more than three times the size of the White House in Washington, D.C.

The modern architecture made sure to retain a certain touch of Kazakh culture and style, which is now combined into this futuristic yet traditional "Kazakhi way." The combination of big, bright, functional, and encouraging offers a window into the soul of this country and into the direction in which the Nazarbayev administration intends to go. This neo-Kazakh design is in a certain manner a reflection of the Kazakh identity President Nazarbayev is trying to forge out of the multitude of nationalities and ethnic groups found in the country.

149

"The character of Kazakhstan is similar to our huge territory and also our character; it is open and inviting," Tugzhanov told me. The administration of President Nazarbayev has invested much in building the city and building the Kazakh society out of the several dozens of different groups who live here. There is a sense one gets that the president is almost obsessed as to the manner in which history will remember him.

That is not at all unusual with elder statesmen when they reach a certain point in their career, or when they get to be a certain age, or both. They sit back and reflect on how the history books will treat them, and many wish they could do it all over again. Nazarbayev is seventy-one years old and at a certain point in his career, and he is no doubt beginning to wonder how he will be remembered. But he does not have to wish he could do it again because he has already been given a second chance. I don't believe there are many world leaders who can claim to have had the same luck as Nazarbayev by getting to run the same country twice; once under Communism and now as a democratic state. In that regard, Nazarbayev could not be luckier. He gets a second chance at running the same country under a different regime, only this time he gets to do it right. This time everyone wants to be his friend and everyone wants him to succeed. It's not every world leader who gets a chance to go from being secretary general of the Communist party of a Soviet Socialist republic to becoming the president of a democratic country and a member and chairperson of the OSCE, or who gets to shift his country's policies from being a member of the Warsaw Pact nations (as part of the USSR) to joining NATO affiliates. That in itself is quite an accomplishment. This time he gets more money (both for himself and for the country) to do the same job, but with more benefits. This time he gets the support of both his former master in Moscow and of his onetime foe, now very good friend, the United States. This time he has oil and gas.

Oil and gas are the leaders of Kazakhstan's economy. Natural gas production amounted to 16.6 billion cubic meters in 2007.[2] It is estimated that the country's recoverable oil reserves stand at about 4 billion tons, while the gas reserves are 3 trillion cubic meters. Future market analysis predicts that the planned expansion of oil fields, along with new fields coming on line, should enable Kazakhstan to produce as much as 3 million barrels a day by 2015. This would place Kazakhstan among the world's top ten oil-producing nations.

Some of the president's critics have accused him of promoting a personality cult, with his pictures appearing everywhere from magazine and book covers to roadside billboards. In a Western culture, it is seen as going over the top. But one has to understand that this is not the West and that there is a different culture where this is almost expected. Anyway, promoting the president's ego is not the worst thing that can happen to the country.

During the time I spent in Kazakhstan I began to look closely at some of the president's initiatives, and I became convinced that he truly cares for his people. He is genuinely concerned for their welfare. Indeed he has accomplished much, but he is particularly pleased by the fact that Kazakhstan was awarded the chair of the OSCE for a year. He now hopes he can leave a lasting impression on the future.

But what will be the legacy Nazarbayev leaves behind? Is it the new capital city? Is it the new notion of nationality? Is it his efforts to curb the proliferation of religion as a weapon of mass seduction by Islamists? Or is he more likely to be remembered for giving up his country's nuclear weapons? Or perhaps he will be remembered for his initiatives in preventing terrorism and promoting interfaith understanding and tolerance? I believe Nazarbayev will be remembered for a little bit of each of the above-mentioned topics.

When you consider all that the president has contributed in placing Kazakhstan on the map—and in a positive manner—all in all this is not a bad report card by which to be remembered. Well, except for the continued reminders about human rights abuses.

During one of my many long conversations with several top officials who were kind enough to give me their time and explain to me how things worked in the country and why they worked in that manner, information without which I could have never written this book, I asked a close advisor of the president if there was one particular person in history whom Nazarbayev looked up to or who had impressed the president in his younger days? The reply was, yes, there is: Nazarbayev is impressed by Atatürk.

An interesting choice, I thought. There are indeed numerous similarities that jump to mind, not least starting with the fact that Atatürk is Turkish and Nazarbayev is Turkic. The Kazakh president's detractors have a field day making light of the matter whenever either the president himself or someone else makes the comparison, but I think it is rather appropriate.

When Mustafa Kemal Atatürk set out to modernize Ottoman Turkey, doing away with the caliphate and creating the modern Turkish Republic, he believed that Turkey's future would be far sturdier if it were anchored in Europe rather than looking toward the Levant,[3] the Hijaz,[4] and Central Asia, as it had done in the past.

In this regard Kazakhstan is at a slight geographic disadvantage from Turkey, which at least has a part of its territory physically situated in Europe, small as it may be. Kazakhstan on the other hand is separated from Europe geographically, but still remains attached to Europe sentimentally, as was discussed earlier.

Atatürk also firmly believed that religion should not be mixed with politics and felt so strongly about it that he borrowed a word from French—*laïcité*—to stress that he intended for Turkey's separation of mosque and state to be far more than secular. This is a sentiment mirrored by Nazarbayev in Kazakhstan, who made sure that when the constitution was written in 1993 and amended in 1995 it was made very clear that there was no room in Kazakh politics for religious parties.

Kazakhstan had taken matters a step further than Turkey, where the current ruling party, the prime minister's Justice and Development Party (AKP) is an Islamist party. This could never happen in Kazakhstan, at least not as long as the current constitution is in effect.

Atatürk wanted to make Turkey into a European nation. He changed the alphabet from Arabic script to Latin. He banned the veil for women (the first notion of Islam without a veil?) and the fez or *tarboush* for men, and introduced and encouraged Western dress.

You can rest assured that there was much opposition to his ideas. How he dealt with that opposition is not something that the history books dwell on at any great length. Of course there was no instant media and no Internet at the time to report his every move, and human rights groups were not present to defend those whose rights may have been ignored and trampled. But would it have been possible for Turkey to undergo those changes—that quantum jump in political and social architecture—had Atatürk not proceeded in the manner he did?

Atatürk had a vision for his country that placed it apart and ahead of its time and its contemporaries and took Turkey on a path to economic and political stability that the country would have never seen otherwise. He aligned Turkey with the world's new rising power, the Western Alliance, positioning his country as Western Europe's (and later NATO's) first line of defense against the Soviet Union and Warsaw Pact countries. Just emerging from the defeat of World War I, Atatürk's task—and his vision for a modern Turkey—was larger than life. But then again, so was the man.

If in later years Turkey faced economic hardships and experienced political turbulence with the rule of democracy interrupted three times—in 1961, 1970, and 1980—it was through no fault of Atatürk's. He laid the groundwork and handed over the state to his political heirs. How they proceeded from that point onward was beyond his control. He had, however, built a safety net with a strong military that restored order every time.

In looking at the achievements made by Kazakhstan under the leadership of President Nazarbayev in the same political, social, economic, and religious fields, one cannot help but notice the striking similarities that jump out when compared to Atatürk.

Both men had dreams that to the majority of people would appear inconceivable, but as the motto of the British Special Air Services (SAS) goes, "He who dares, wins." Indeed, both Atatürk and Nazarbayev dared, and both men won. What these two men also had in common was their strong desire to serve their country in a positive manner and to leave behind a lasting legacy. "He has trust in the people," said Yeraly Tugzhanov, the vice chairman of the Kazakhstan Assembly, speaking of his president.

One can criticize both leaders for their spirit of grandeur and accuse them of having inflated egos and such, and it may well be true. Many world leaders are very likely to have big egos; it's just that some hide it better than others. But if you want to really understand these men and how they think, you need to study them on their own ground. These leaders should be looked at with local lenses and not through American or European eyes. What will emerge will be a very different picture.

Both Atatürk and Nazarbayev had countries with a multitude of nationalities and ethnicities. Turkey had several important minorities: Kurds, Circassians, and Armenians. Kazakhstan has considerably more. And both countries wanted to create a feeling of national pride and of national belonging through the notion of the nation, not through religion.

Prior to that change one was a Turk by birth, a Muslim by religion, or a Greek who lived in Turkey. This caused divisions among the people and Atatürk made it so that—no matter his or her origins—as long as one wanted to become a Turk, he or she could. This gave the people a greater sense of belonging and created a national pride in being Turkish. Nazarbayev is attempting to do the same in Kazakhstan.

They both thrived to work for the benefit of the entire country and for the good of the entire population, not just to advance a single ethnic group or any one religion at the detriment of others. And both men were able to realize those dreams. Atatürk, much as Nazarbayev, inherited a country in less-than-perfect shape economically, and then turned the country around into a modern and vibrant society with a stable economy and a solid political base that made his country into a regional power.

Atatürk found himself at the helm of Turkey after its defeat in World War I with an economy in terrible shape and the problems that come associated with post-war struggles. Not to mention, of course, the objections that must have accompanied his political views and his intentions to completely transform Turkey in just about every possible perspective: the social, educational, political, and economic facets of life in the country, and, not to be underestimated, a very important component in a Muslim country, religion.

Likewise, Nazarbayev, although he was already at the helm of Kazakhstan as the head of the Kazakhstan Communist Party when his country was jettisoned from the Soviet system into a free market economy, adopted a similar vision of greatness for his country. Nazarbayev's view of keeping Kazakhstan a secular state is very similar to what Atatürk had in mind for Turkey. Both men realized that if their countries were to advance in business and politics and attempt to keep up with modern times and keep pace with the changing world, especially as part of Europe (for Turkey) and as a partner of Europe and the United States (for Kazakhstan), they had to keep religion and politics well apart, or else their vision of a modern nation could never see the light of day.

There is a saying that you don't make an omelet without breaking a few eggs. In a similar manner, you don't build a democracy without breaking some of the very laws you are trying to instill in a society. Keep in mind that not all societies are similar and react the same way to change. Remember that change brings conflict and some societies are reluctant to accept or even to attempt change.

Remember that what Atatürk did was a phenomenon. Not only did he change the political system and transform the country from an Islamic caliphate into a Western-styled democracy, he changed the way people lived, the way they wrote, and the way they read, among many other changes. And he came out looking like a hero.

Turkey may well have a multitude of political parties today, covering the gamut of the political spectrum from the far left to the far right and all that is in between, but it is worth recalling that when Atatürk created the new Turkish state, there was but a single party. Kazakhstan has ten political parties.[5]

Installing democracy in Europe and North America (a place where the majority of the population are of European heritage) is very different from installing democracy in Central Asia or the Middle East, where there is not the same historic attachment to democracy. It would not be fair to hold both societies to the same standard. Each society must be judged according to the environment and trends that influence that society today. As President Nazarbayev told me in an interview last year, it is not up to the West to set the standards of democracy.

Nazarbayev said that he did not necessarily agree with the stance that the Western way of life and views should be "the ultimate truth." He spoke of domestic and cultural factors that one needs to take into consideration, and this is something the West typically forgets.

Other similarities between the first president of the modern Turkish state and the first president of the modern Kazakh state include the following: Both elected to move the country's capital city; Atatürk designated Ankara as his new capital after basing his troops there during the foreign occupation of the former capital, Istanbul. He then decided to maintain the capital in Ankara, which is in the heart of Anatolia, in the very center of the country. Nazarbayev also decided to designate a new capital, Astana, and transferred all government functions from Almaty almost a decade ago.

There are no official versions of why the change was made, though there are three unofficial versions—take your pick. The first story goes that the government of Kazakhstan did not particularly like the notion that they were sitting less than an hour's drive from the Chinese border. Astana is considerably farther north and closer to Russia than China. The second reason is that Almaty is situated in an earthquake zone and the president did not think it would be wise to retain the government there. And the third reason is that the president wanted to leave behind him a living legacy, an entire city. His city, Astana.

As to the question of whether there is the possibility of democracy and Islam coexisting, the answer I will give here has already been confirmed in the last few pages you have just read by two prominent figures in our modern contemporary history: Mustafa Kemal Atatürk and Nursultan Nazarbayev.

Islam and democracy can coexist, with certain caveats. First there has to be mutual respect for one another. That means that religion must not interfere in politics and politics must stay out of religion. If that cardinal rule can be met, then by all means there should be no reason for contention between the two. But if religion continues to meddle in politics there will be a great amount of difficulty getting the two to agree on anything, and then we may well be heading for that clash of civilizations that has been so widely talked about.

Politics and religion must be separated and kept apart. In studying the difference in attitude, education level, productivity, and all other aspects of life, it quickly becomes obvious that in order to succeed in just about every field, from business to entertainment, not being burdened by religious dogma allows for a better productive state.

Still the question remains: Can Islam coexist with democracy? Yes, of course it can, but it needs to remain away from politics. This is the time to enact changes and not procrastinate, as eventually time will run out. We have seen democracy interact very positively with Islam in Turkey, we have seen it coexist and prosper in Kosovo, and we are seeing it work extremely well in Kazakhstan. There is no reason on earth why the Kazakh model that has proven to be so successful cannot be replicated and exported to other Muslim countries.

The only barrier that exists between Muslims and non-Muslims, or yet between Muslims and Christians and Jews, is a mental barrier, a mental wall that was erected by people who fear change. To all those who believe that Islam cannot coexist in peace with democracy and with other religions, "tear down this (mental) wall."

THIRTEEN

A Conversation with a Salafi

"All that is necessary for the triumph of evil is that good men do nothing."

—*Edmund Burke, Anglo-Irish statesman*

inding a *Salafi* in Saudi Arabia is a relatively simple task: just walk into any mosque on any given day and chances are there will be a number of them right there in the first row of the faithful. Finding one in Kazakhstan is a tad harder. *Salafis* are not as visible or nearly as numerous as the ones in Saudi Arabia, and Kazakhstan would like to keep it that way.

However, they do exist in this Central Asian republic and I finally succeeded in meeting a young Kazakh *Salafi*. Despite monumental efforts by the authorities to keep the country as secular as possible, there are nonetheless a certain number of them here.

Most *Salafis* in Kazakhstan, according to the grand mufti, come here from Saudi Arabia, and they hope to "convert" Kazakh Muslims to *Salafism*. According to this young man, Yusef, there are several thousands like him in Kazakhstan, and he says the numbers are growing.

This is certainly not something the government wants to hear. But it is something they are, no doubt, looking into, if there is any truth to that statement. Kazakh security forces remain extremely vigilant, particularly when it comes to anything having to do with the Islamists. Nobody here in Kazakhstan wants to see some of the problems their neighbors are facing from Islamist groups. The thrust of the president's program, as we have seen, is to keep the country secular and keep the Islamists away.

I met Yusef during my last week in Astana, as I was wrapping up a marathon month of interviews before dashing back to my apartment to punch out my notes into something that would make sense and then sitting down to write about one to two thousand words a day, trying to cram as much as humanly possible into a twenty-four-hour period.

Yusef was a bright young man in his twenties, a fourth-generation Kazakh of Kurdish origin, and a *Salafi*. He was about to leave Kazakhstan for a four-year stint in the City of Mecca in Saudi Arabia to study the Holy Quran. The young man was eager to share his knowledge of Islam and *Salafism* with me. He came over with some friends to the apartment I was renting during my stay in Kazakhstan and we spent several hours discussing religion, mainly Islam, of course, but we also touched upon Christianity in general, and naturally I had to interject Catholicism in the process.

The conversation unfolded mainly in Arabic, though at times Yusef would switch to Russian, which my friend Alibek Kimanov and his charming wife, Lyazzat, would graciously translate into English. Following the traditional greetings and exchanges of general information about ourselves, Yusef started out by saying that he liked Islam because Muslims believe in one God and that he knew that Islam is the true religion.

I told him that the very same concept applies to Christians, and that Christians also believe in one God. I added that the Christian God is the very same God as the God of the Muslims, except you call him Allah and Christians call him God and the Jews call him Yahweh. But the Arabic word for God is Allah, and Arab Christians pray to Allah.

Allah is not only the God of Islam, he is the one and only God that the "People of the Book," Jews, Christians, and Muslims, revere. Allah is recognized in the West as the God of Islam, but Mizrahi Jews also use the term Allah, as do the Baha'i and Christians of the Eastern Orthodox Church. The word Allah is derived from the combination of the article *al*, meaning "the," and the contraction of the word *illahi*, meaning "my God."

"No," said Yusef, "Christians pray to three Gods. You pray to God, you pray to Jesus, et cetera." Ah, the great mystery of the Holy Trinity. I tried conjuring up memories from Catechism classes at the Catholic schools I attended that are stashed away in some deep, dark, forgotten corner of my brain. I now wished I had paid more attention and engaged in less daydreaming. Where is Father Bias when you need him?

This, I told Yusef, is the mystery of the Holy Trinity. I tried to explain that there are three persons within one God: God the Father, God the Son, and God the Holy Spirit. This is something that even after eight years of Catholic schools I still do not comprehend fully, and I don't think I was making much headway, especially as I was trying to carry on the conversation in Arabic, touching upon a topic I had never before discussed in Arabic.

If you are Catholic you simply have to accept the notion of the Holy Trinity as one of the unexplainable mysteries that make the religion what it is. As the Church would probably say if you were to pry for a more logical explanation, "Don't ask and we will not tell." Christians have only one God, I tried to reassure Yusef.

"But what about Mariam; is she not God?" he asked. The Virgin Mary is another of the Catholic Church's mysteries. The Immaculate Conception and the virgin birth, along with the Holy Spirit, are questions without logical answers for mere mortals such as ourselves. Again, this is one of those package deals where you simply have to take the Church's word for it. This is where you either have faith or you don't have faith. Muslims, by the way, accept Jesus, whom they call Issa, as a prophet and honor him accordingly.[1] They just don't believe he is God.

I told Yusef that, in fact, if you read the New Testament carefully, nowhere do you find Jesus ever saying he is God. When Jesus chases the moneychangers out of the temple in Jerusalem, he accuses them of soiling his father's house. As we are all supposed to be the children of God, Jesus certainly had the right to say that God was his father. When he is put on trial and asked by the Romans if he was truly the son of God, Jesus replied that he was the son of man.

As for Yusef's statement that Islam was the true religion, I asked Yusef how did he know that he knew the truth? I repeated to him what I had told my Palestinian students in Gaza a few years ago about the truth.

You are convinced that you have an absolute handle on the truth, you are so certain of knowing without an ounce of doubt in your mind that you know the truth. Fine. Now, I feel exactly the same. I know that what I know is the truth. For me there is also not a shadow of a doubt that I am correct. So which one of us is the holder of the truth?

Now, before you answer that question, think first before you say that you are the one with the true answer. Let us first analyze what is truth. One definition of the truth is given as such: "That which is true in accordance with fact or reality." Another definition is: "A fact or belief that is accepted as true."[2]

Let us begin with the first definition. Something that is true in accordance with fact or reality. Once again, I will suggest that what is fact for you may not qualify as fact for me. And the same applies with reality. You and I live in completely separate worlds. We cannot possibly arrive at the same facts and the same realities.

As for the second definition, a fact or belief that is accepted as true—well, first of all, I may not accept your facts, and a belief is just as the word defines it, a belief. You believe in God. That is a fact, but if I were to play devil's advocate, I could counter by saying that while there is no question about your believing is God, nor is there any doubt regarding your faith, is there concrete evidence that there is a God?

Yusef was not terribly convinced. I asked Yusef if he knew the words of the *Shahada*,[3] also called the *Kalima*.[4] Of course he knew the lines of the *Shahada*. I had no doubt that he did, but I recited them to him nonetheless: *Bismillah al-Rahman al-Rahim, ash-had enu la Illahi il-Allah, wa Muhammad Rasul Allah.* (In the name of God the most gracious and most merciful, I swear that I have no other gods but God, and that Mohammad is God's messenger.)

I asked if he knew the words of the first *surah* or chapter of the Holy Quran, which of course he did: *Bismillah al-Rahman al-Rahim, al-hamdu l'Illahi, Rab el aalamin . . .* (In the name of God the most compassionate, the merciful. Praise be to God, Lord of the Worlds. The compassionate, the merciful. Master of Judgment Day. You alone we worship, and to You alone we pray for help. Guide us to the straight path. The path of those whom You have favored. Not of those who have incurred Your wrath, not of those who have gone astray.)

Yusef nodded; those were the correct words for the first *surah*. There are far more similarities between the Islam and Christianity than you care to realize, I said. I asked Yusef if he knew the First, Second and Third Commandments of the Ten Commandments? That he did not know, so I told him.

The First Commandment: I am the Lord your God, who brought you out of the land of Egypt, out of the house of bondage. Thou shall have no other gods before me. The Second Commandment: You shall not make for yourself any carved image, or any likeness of anything that is in heaven above, or that is in the earth beneath, or that is in the water under the earth; you shall not bow down to them nor serve them. For I, the Lord your God, am a jealous God, visiting the iniquity of the fathers on the children to the third and fourth generations of those who hate me, but showing mercy to thousands, to those who love Me and keep My commandments. The Third Commandment: You shall not take the name of the Lord your God in vain, for the Lord will not hold him guiltless who takes His name in vain.

From there we moved on to another topic. I asked Yusef what he knew about the *Takfiri* movement and what he thought of them. He didn't have to be asked twice. He instantly lashed out at them, saying that not everything was right up there, pointing his finger to his head.

"If you are supposed to pray five times a day and for some reason you miss one of the five calls to prayer *Takfiris* will say you are *kufr*, not *kafir*, but k*ufr*. A *kafir* is an unbeliever, whereas a *kufr* is a sin," explained Yusef. "They call you a sin, not a sinner, but a sin, if you miss one prayer. If you were to worship a cow instead of Allah that would not make you a sin. But in the eyes of the *Takfiris* that is enough to label someone a sin."

The young *Salafi* stated that he did not agree with the *Takfiri* beliefs and their use of violence. "It's alright for *Takfiris* to kill someone because they disagree with him. That is not the true way of Islam. Islam is first and foremost a religion of peace. Islam means to surrender completely to Allah. Jihad, the meaning of the word jihad has been completely distorted by the *Takfiri* movement. Jihad begins with oneself. What they are doing is not the way of Islam," said Yusef.

"The holy wars that the children of Adam are waging today are not true holy wars. Taking other lives is not jihad. We will have to answer for that kind of jihad when we are questioned in the grave," writes the Sufi master, Muhaiyaddeen.[5]

Indeed one could not possibly have two more opposing philosophies and different interpretations of the Quran and the Hadith than what comes to us from the Sufis and the *Takfiris*. On the one hand, *Takfiris* advocate violence as a means of achieving their goals. If it means using suicide bombers, if it means flying commercial airplanes filled with passengers into office buildings, and if it means beheading one's enemies, so be it.

This is what Sufism has to say about jihad: "Praising Allah and then destroying others is not jihad. Some groups wage war against the children of Adam and call it jihad, but for man to raise his sword against man, for man to kill man, is not jihad."[6]

I asked Yusef what he wanted to be when he completed his studies in four years. He said he had no idea. But what will he be able to do filled with knowledge of the Quran and practically nothing else? This young man is representative of whole generations of young Muslims who are being trained to recite the Quran by heart, which is perfect and very impressive if you want to be a cleric. But a lively society needs more that smart clerics.

Yusef, and I am sure that the same applies to all those like him who aspire to follow the curricula of Quranic schools, lives in such a world apart, totally secluded from reality, so consumed by his religious studies, so isolated from the realities of everyday life, that he has no time for anything else.

I had already heard all of what Yusef had to say before. Not from Yusef, but from others very much like him. I had heard it in Egypt, I heard it in Saudi Arabia, I heard it in Gaza, and in a number of countries where similar ideas exist. The recitation, the dialogue, and the rhetoric is so similar that one can only summarize that these institutions are producing class after class of automatons who think uniformly, with not one ever daring to think outside the box.

This is so contradictory to what centers of higher education aspire to accomplish by stimulating the mind and encouraging students to think differently, to question everything time and again, to take nothing for granted.

How does a society establish centers of scientific research under such circumstances? (It doesn't.) How does a society keep up with inventions or breakthroughs in medicine if all studies are focused in the same direction, without diverging a single iota from century to century? (It doesn't.) If the *Salafis* and *Takfiris* oppose all forms of modernity, then they should go all the way. They should forgo all air transportation. They should turn in their cellular telephones. They should avoid all forms of motorized transportation, from the moped to the car to truck and water transport. They should cancel their Internet subscriptions and give up their e-mail accounts and close down their thousands of Internet websites.

Yusef had no idea what the Gaza Strip was or where it is when I mentioned it to him. He had no idea of what the West Bank was. I mentioned Hamas, an

Islamist movement, and I got a blank stare. And that was not due to something lost in translation, because I had our mutual friend Alibek repeat in
Russian what I had said in Arabic. He had never heard the Arabic term for
Christian, *Messihi*, used before. Yet he spoke excellent Arabic and was able to
read and write it. He used the word *Nasrani*, instead.[7]

But he could quote from the Holy Book of Islam without hesitation. And
I'm quite sure by the time he is done with his studies four years from now he
will be able to quote entire pages from the Hadith, as well as the *Sunnah*. If
that is the level of learning that the *Salafi* education will provide, then expect
the next major UN report on the state of affairs in the Arab/Muslim world to
regress even more.

If the current trend continues with emphasis placed on religion instead
of contemporary education, then expect the gap within the Muslim world, as
well as the gap between Islam and the rest of the world, to grow exponentially.
There is a real danger that if this trend is allowed to continue unchecked it
could lead to a real clash between the West and Islam, even if those concerned
are only a small minority.

The vast majority of Muslims are regular folks who want to go about their
business, who want to raise their families, and who want to live in peace like
most other people. The danger arises from the few vociferous extremists who
are giving the whole religion a bad name and risking drawing the majority
down with them.

Already there are numerous reports that the situation for women in the
Central Asian country of Uzbekistan has regressed since the days of the Soviet
Union. During the last years there have been hundreds of reports of doctors
performing forced sterilization because of government pressure, according to
reports from human rights groups and health officials. Among the hundreds
of reports of forced sterilization emerging from victims, those who are the
most targeted are low-income Uzbek women. Doctors have been targeting
women with HIV, tuberculosis, or drug addiction, and according to press
reports, often the instruments used for the procedures are not sterile, placing
the women in grave danger.[8] Some reports even say that some employers will
require a certificate of sterilization before giving a woman a job. And if the
fundamentalists ever get their way you can expect women's rights to deteriorate even further.

This is why so much emphasis is being placed on making sure that the Islamists in Afghanistan do not get the upper hand. I believe Dr. Cohen of the Heritage Foundation in Washington is on the mark when he says that such an outcome would be disastrous for everyone.

With all of the above in mind, the reasons countries like Kazakhstan are pushing for good education and separation between religion and politics become all the more evident. In Kazakhstan President Nazarbayev understands very well where this is likely to go and the harm it could cause to his country and the region if the extremists get their way.

The relevant question here is whether this problem is becoming evident to only one side, or will the fundamentalists begin to see the results of their philosophy, and if not, will they continue to live in the past? Will they ever come to agree that reform is badly needed to enhance the needs of their society?

Opposition to change in Islam is going to be strong, even among the young. One bright young female student from the Eurasia University in Astana where I was invited to speak during my last visit to Kazakhstan objected to the idea of introducing any change in any religion because, she said, "It would alter the religion, something that would go against the will of God." As to who gave her a direct line of communication with God remains to be seen.

What she ignored is that in order to survive, a religion needs to evolve. If it remains still in time it will eventually become a thing of the past. Of course the current continued growth of Islam proves my last statement completely wrong; there is a very logical explanation for that, for the Muslim world in general, but this applies particularly more to the Arab world.

The rise of Islam for the most part can be credited to current political trends. In the Arab world, for example, there is not one single popular leader for the people to look up to. There is no Nasser,[9] there is no Boumediène,[10] and there is no Aflaq or Bitar.[11] And with all due respect to King Abdullah of Saudi Arabia, much as he would like to become "the next Nasser," he simply lacks the charisma, the oratory skills, and the ability to manipulate the masses. Additionally, the Saudis come with a lot of baggage. But one area where change is going to take root is on the secular front with change being demanded by the young people in the Arab world. We have already seen the result of such changes in Tunisia and Egypt, where presidents Zein El Abidine Ben Ali and Hosni Mubarak were forced out of office by popular demonstrations. In any case Egypt's Mubarak was not very much liked and had zero charisma, and King Abdullah II of Jordan is still too young. And although I have a tremendous amount of personal respect and admiration for the Hashemite monarch, he has the disadvantage of being the king of Jordan—the other countries in the region will never allow Jordan to lead the Arab world.

The Arab world has been orphaned of any real charismatic leadership with the disappearance of those just named, not that they were great examples of democracy. Anwar Sadat, who followed Nasser, could have been a great pan-Arab leader, but his visit to Jerusalem to address the Israeli Knesset cost him whatever charisma he had, and it ultimately cost him his life. He was assassinated by a member of the Muslim Brotherhood as he watched a military parade on October 6, 1981, on the anniversary of the October 1973 War.

The lack of any real leadership in the Arab world since the 1970s explains the shift from popular politics to popular religion in the region. This is owing to the fact that political leaders in the region promoted themselves rather than their ideas, so their political movements largely disappeared with them. A perfect example of this is how a large part of the rank and file of the Palestinian Islamic Resistance Movement, Hamas, comes from the Popular Front for the Liberation of Palestine, a Marxist group who was very active in the late 1960s, '70s, and '80s. But with the death of its leader, George Habbash, the movement has practically disappeared.

Today the Arab world is turning to non-Arab Muslim leaders for direction, such as Iranian president Mahmoud Ahmadinejad and Turkey's prime minister Recep Tayyip Erdogan. Even Syrian president Bashar Assad acknowledged as much when he told the visiting Turkish leader that he was more popular among Syrians than the Syrian president.

This is not an attempt by the Western world to dominate Muslim society. This is an honest cri de coeur from an observer of history who had the great privilege of living in both cultures, of growing up in both cultures, and of learning to understand the greatness—and the weakness—of both cultures. This is an attempt from someone who truly cares deeply for both cultures. From my vantage point as a journalist, I can clearly see the great similarities between the different cultures and religions, especially among "The People of the Book," who share a common heritage, all three being descendents of Abraham, or Ibrahim in Arabic.

Whether reform on a major scale as suggested in the pages of this book will ever become a reality is not a given. Whether any reform at all can be pushed through remains to be seen. The situation is nothing less than critical and it has been recognized to be critical by, among others, Kazakhstan and its president. That is the reason for all of the interfaith conferences the Kazakhs have hosted. That is the reason the Kazakhs keep investing in the prevention of terrorism. If the current educational gap continues to grow, there will come a time in the not-too-distant future when the gap will be so wide, so distant, that catching up will take decades, if not more.

Meanwhile, the moderate countries like Kazakhstan, Jordan, Syria (from a secular point of view), Malaysia, and others will continue to send their children to foreign universities to pursue a good higher education. But the gap between those who have studied abroad and the rest becomes so pronounced that the brain drain begins to become problematic for the countries in question.

The best and the brightest end up emigrating to the United States, or to Canada, or to Europe. Kazakhstan has tried to protect itself from that by having the students sent abroad at the state's expense sign a waiver stating they will return. Failing that, the student's parents are obliged to reimburse the state at a very high interest rate. Kazakh culture and the respect of the family do not permit the students to forgo their agreements.

Will the conservative branches of Islam ever reach the point where they will begin to consider the need for change? Will we live to see the kinder, gentler, and more humane face of Islam eventually emerge and take control of the religion? Will Islam without a veil ever become a reality, other than in Kazakhstan? *Insha'Allah.*

FOURTEEN

Is a Middle East and Central Asia Economic Common Market Possible?

"There are two primary choices in life: to accept conditions as they exist, or accept the responsibility for changing them."

—Denis Waitley, motivational speaker

The problems facing the Muslim world today come under two principal headings: the issues emanating from the Arab world and those concerning Central Asian countries. They each contribute in making the Muslim world a little less safe and they all contribute in emphasizing that the violent wing of Islam is contradictory to the very nature of what a Muslim is meant to be.

The bottom line is that these problems, be they in Central Asia or the Middle East, must not be ignored, as they have a tendency of feeding on themselves and then spiraling out of control. A good example is the Arab-Israeli conflict, which in fact should no longer be called that; instead it should be called the Arab-Israeli-Turkish-Iranian crisis. Though it may not be, it appears to be at the center of every other problem touching the Middle East and Central Asia today. Remember bin Laden and his claims that he had carried out the 9/11 attacks partially as revenge against what the Israelis are doing to the Palestinians?

Yet, if the countries in question in the greater Middle East and Central Asia were ever able to reach political maturity on the level of the European

Union, for example, the combined potential of the region would have the makings of a superpower on a par with the United States, if not even greater. Those who use violence so prominently in Islam today must learn to conduct negotiations through dialogue rather than through bombs.

The Soviet Union had nuclear weapons and was the second superpower in the world, and still, none of that helped it very much. Not its hundreds of nukes, not its formidable army, not the buffer of its satellite states—none of that was able to save it because Moscow ignored one fundamental and all-powerful weapon, a weapon the United States and Europe used only too well against the Soviets. The weapon was the economy.

Now perhaps it becomes somewhat clearer why President Nazarbayev of Kazakhstan keeps insisting so much on fixing the economy before allowing greater political freedom in his country. He has seen how devastating poor economic policies can be and the havoc they can wreck on a country, even if the country is a superpower armed with nuclear weapons and with territory stretching from the Arctic to the Pacific and from the Baltics practically to the Persian Gulf.

The Soviets ignored the economic angle and that's where they lost.

Throughout this book I have drawn analogies between Communism and militant Islam. Well, here's another one: Just as the economy was the downfall of the Soviet Union, so, too, will it affect the Islamists who continue to place emphasis on violence in an effort to promote their narrow vision of religion, rather than looking at the bottom line. Not God, not religion, but the economy drives the world today.

Those who believe that the United States can be defeated militarily are very wrong and should not be fooled by Iraq, Afghanistan, or even Vietnam. If the immediate security of the United States is at stake the U.S. military has weapons at its disposal that were never used, and hopefully never will be used. The United States still has the world's largest and most powerful military and the best hardware and armament for the individual soldier, sailor, airman, and Marine. Anyone planning to take on the United States from a military perspective is simply unrealistic.

So think economics and move away from dead-end politics that have only brought your country strife and internal dissent and the fear of a constant coup forcing you to rule accordingly. Just how much fun is that?

Now imagine, if you will, if all the countries in the Middle East and all the countries of Central Asia were able to resolve their main issues and get along the way the Europeans do. Imagine if Syria and Israel had the same type of relations France and Germany enjoy today.

You think that is hard to imagine? Look at Europe: How many wars were fought between France and Germany? Between France and England? Between Germany and Russia? Between the Austro-Hungarians and their neighbors? How many armies waltzed across Poland and how many times were the borders shifted, redrawn, and shifted back? Look at Europe today. Twenty-seven nations speaking twenty-three different languages as diverse as French, Lithuanian, Hungarian, and Maltese, practicing dozens of different religions, but united in the single largest economic market in the world with a single currency, the euro, worth more than the U.S. dollar today.

The Middle East and Central Asia have it much easier. There are basically two languages, Arabic and Russian, and one religion, Islam. Granted, there are important Christian minorities to consider, as well as important linguistic minorities in the region.

War in Europe today is simply unimaginable because the EU has intertwined the economies of its member states in such a manner that it is simply unthinkable for any two members to resort to armed conflict any longer. It just cannot happen. So imagine a similar political climate developing in the Middle East and Central Asia, where tourists arrive by cruise liner to Beirut or Haifa and board a rapid train that takes them all the way to Tashkent, Bishkek, and beyond.

Imagine if commercial airliners could land with equal ease in Baghdad, Tehran, Tel Aviv, Kabul, and Peshawar, where they could pick up and drop off passengers without having to worry about boycott laws. And the only boom would be an economic one. Imagine for a brief moment how the region would look if the standard of living were raised a few notches. Think how much better off the daily laborer in Egypt or Kyrgyzstan would be if he could bring home a few dollars more to feed his family. Think how the dynamics of Egyptian politics and how Kyrgyz politics would be affected.

Picture the results of a vast industrialized zone established in Gaza or in Dushanbe, where labor is abundant, easy to train, and inexpensive—and where European and U.S. car manufacturers can open assembly plants and textile mills to market their products in the Middle East, Africa, Central Asia, and beyond. Envision the Middle East and Central Asia without refugees. Envision Iraqis returning to normal life. Envision the people of Afghanistan living a normal life. Give the people a taste of what life should be like, make them a little bit more comfortable, and then see how many volunteers for martyrdom still line up for suicide missions. My guess is not so many.

Look at all the natural resources the region has to offer: oil and natural gas, uranium and phosphates, gold and plutonium, and manpower. This is how you dominate the world, through the purse, not by setting off bombs in train and subway stations at rush hour or flying civilian aircrafts into office towers. That is barbarism.

What level of education would you have if you invested the billions of dollars that are spent every year on weapons systems, or on building armies that will never fight. Imagine if that energy and those resources went toward establishing centers of higher education and investing in scientific and medical research.

Think how much richer the area would be intellectually if all the best brains remained in the region, rather than immigrating to North America, Europe, or Australia.

There is a solution to every problem and to every conflict. Making peace with one's enemy requires courage, while remaining in a state of war is far easier because it does not require any change.

The problems touching the Middle East and Central Asia are not to be underestimated by any means. Some of these problems date back more than six decades, yet they become more and more complicated every year, as the Arab-Israeli dispute. Attempting to solve all these problems at once is, of course, unrealistic. However, all these problems have the same underlying current: In one way or another they all have to do with a segment of Islam.

In brief there are a number of issues that continue to raise concern and generate violence and direct hate at the United States. Among them are: 1) the Arab-Israeli conflict; 2) the aftereffects of the U.S. invasion of Iraq; 3) the political morass in Lebanon; and 4) Syria's continued militancy and continued state of war with Israel.

The issues affecting the stability of Central Asia are: 1) the continued mayhem in Afghanistan; 2) continued efforts by Iran to acquire nuclear technology; 3) political instability in Pakistan; and 4) political unrest in Kyrgyzstan.

What is the common denominator in all the problems mentioned above? It appears to be Islam—the violent form of Islam. Is there a quick fix for these problems? A quick fix, I would say, is unlikely. These are issues that will take years to fix, given the level of mistrust that exists today between the two sides.

When my first book came out, I was being interviewed on a local radio station and we were discussing the Middle East and the problems in trying to bring about peace there. As we were getting near the top of the hour and the end of the program, the interviewer turned to me and asked: "Do you think there will ever be peace in the Middle East, and if so, what would be needed for that to happen. In thirty seconds or less, as we have to go to commercial break."

In thirty seconds or less . . . I replied: "I do believe there will be peace in the Middle East and that will happen the day that the antagonists develop greater love for their children than hate for their enemies."

FIFTEEN

Changin' Times

O ne thing that is certain in today's uncertain world is that Bob Dylan was right. The times they are a-changin'. Dylan's popular song from the 1960s was and still is prophetic. Time is constantly changing to the point that some thinkers have questioned its very existence.

Many are those who would like to stop time in order to avoid change. Others want to speed it up, usually because they don't like the changes taking place at a given time. Regardless of how much the vast majority of people dislike change, fear it, and try everything possible to avoid it in the end, change, much like death and taxes, is inevitable.

Take a good long look around you and take notice, because few things in the world remain stagnant. Look again in five or ten years and you will see a very different landscape from what you just looked at. Much of the world as you know it today will have changed in five to ten years, and then changed some more in fifteen to twenty years, and some of those changes will be radical. Starting with yourself.

Change is all around us. People change; they change the way they comb their hair and the color and style of eyeglasses they wear. They update their wardrobes; they may go for a different color they never considered wearing before. That purple shirt you always wanted to buy but never dared? Go for it! So what if your teenage daughter tells you that you look ridiculous and are making a fool of yourself.

Other people change how they feel about politics. They may change the way they vote. They may go from voting liberal to becoming somewhat more conservative as they grow older. Or it could be that they will go from conservative to liberal, thinking that society needs better social guardrails. They may change their political opinion time and again. Politicians change sides and move from left to right and vice versa.

People may change lovers, wives, or husbands. They may change jobs, or even change careers. They can change their names. They can change homes, move to different cities, even to different countries. They may also change nationalities and pledge allegiance to new nations. They can learn a new language and change the way they speak. They can change cultures or adopt new cultures and become multicultured. They may even change gender or sexual orientation. In today's fast-moving world, all this change is happening more and more frequently.

And countries also change. They change laws. They change their direction in domestic or foreign policy. They may change immigration laws, tax laws, and criminal laws as the need arises. They change governments, prime ministers, and presidents. They change alliances. They change economic and political systems of government.

Look at the countries of the former Soviet system and see the tectonic changes that took place there. Look at Kazakhstan and see how much it has changed in the last twenty years, in only one generation. Kazakhstan went from a Communist system, from being a Soviet Socialist Republic, to taking the fast track to a free-market economy and becoming a pathfinder and leader in Central Asia. It changed from being a member of the Warsaw Pact, countries that trained to attack the West, to joining Western defense organizations.

And what about religion; does it change? Some will tell you no, it remains constant. Well, despite what many people might think, that religion remains the same, that at least something in this world remains constant, everything changes. For those of you who would like to believe that religion is constant, I have bad news, folks: Religion undergoes changes too.

But they will argue that Jews and Christians and Muslims have been praying to God for a couple of millennia. Why try to change things now? Yes, it's true that the manner in which people pray to God has changed very little. But that's not what we want to change. You can pray any way you like.

The Catholic Church introduced some basic changes in the late 1960s to attract more people and to try and stop the exodus of Catholics from the Church. That was when the priest, who until then kept his back turned to the congregation while performing mass, started saying mass facing the congregation. And it was no longer obligatory to say mass in Latin only, but henceforth mass could be recited in any language.

The changes needed are far more profound and whether they undertake to implement these changes or not will affect relations among Muslims and between Muslims and the rest of humanity. If in Islam they have not changed how they pray, they have amended some basic rules in order to allow Muslims to borrow money with interest, giving them the ability to purchase homes in the United States without breaking any religious rules, as usury is banned in Islam. So if you can change the rule on usury you can change the rules regarding other aspects of religion.

Perhaps the manner of change affecting religion is not occurring at the same pace as the rest of the other systems that touch upon religion. But there is no doubt that religion evolves as well, all while keeping its traditions. And that is a good thing, because while people need change they also need continuity, and tradition offers continuity.

Think for example of the many different ways people celebrate traditions. It could be something as simple as a traditional Sunday lunch at the grandparents' house. Or it could be the joyful times of the Eid at the end of the Holy Month of Ramadan for Muslims, and Christmas for Christians, and Chanukah for Jews.

Some religions accept and adapt to change more than others. But given that religion is a living system, it is affected by the interaction of its members and how they in turn interact within the system and outside the system.

For example, relations between two different schools of though such as moderates and *Salafis* (within the system) will impact relations between the system (Islam) and the status of relations with other religions (outside the system). Most systems refuse change when first approached by a new element. When the Prophet first introduced Islam in Arabia he faced stiff opposition from traditionalists who were reluctant to accept the changes. And those changes were drastic when you think about how Islam touched upon every aspect of life.

The Prophet introduced reform that told his followers they should abandon their pagan gods and accept the One God as their God. As John Esposito tells us, the Prophet told his followers to stop the practice of female infanticide; he asked them to show compassion toward the poor; he condemned murder and the lending of money against interest. He introduced the notion that adultery and theft were sins.[1] Muhammad's "insistence that each person was personally accountable not to tribal customary law but to an overriding divine law shook the very foundations of Arabian society."[2]

Jesus Christ was crucified for suggesting changes and reform in Judaism. Let us not forget that the Catholic Church was so worried by change that in the Middle Ages the Church did not encourage the average person to read Scripture. Catholicism, though very conservative in nature, tends to accept change when the Church feels it could face a crisis unless it introduces changes, as with the changes brought about by the Ecumenical Councils.

Islam, or at least certain branches within Islam, tend to be more opposed to change and are willing to fight and to resort to violence to attain their objectives. Yet even those opposed to change the most, the *Takfiri*, will accept changes, often without even realizing it.

In looking at Islam, if you start with the premise that it was a revolution in the sense that the advent of Islam satisfies the definition of the word "revolution"[3] then, much as any other revolution, it needs to continue to make progress, to move forward, or it will slow down, stagnate, and eventually remain running in neutral.

Although Islam is the fastest-growing religion today, one school of thought professes that Islam is a revolution that only partially succeeded as a result of new tensions it brought about when Mohammad introduced the new religion that clashed right away with the "traditionalists who wanted to maintain their old ways." (The first *Salafists?*)

Bernard Lewis, the noted scholar, is of that opinion. By introducing Islam to Arabia, Mohammad completely changed the social and economic structure of Arabian society. Gathering Arabia's warring tribes and uniting them not only into a single religion, Islam, but also into a unified political entity, the Umma, was one of his greatest accomplishments.[4]

Several specialists in Islamic affairs will admit that the Muslim world is changing. It is changing with every major terrorist attack perpetrated by Islamist terrorists. It is changing with every act that depicts Muslims in a negative image. What is happening is that more and more Muslims are beginning to awaken to the fact that no matter who the intended targets of the bombing campaigns happen to be, the ones suffering the most are the regular people.

More and more Muslims seem to be questioning the use of violence to achieve their goals. They are beginning to speak up. They are beginning to stand up and be heard. This happened after September 2001 and it happened after the attack by Chechen Muslim terrorists on a school in Beslan, near Chechnya, where children were the targets.

Religion by its very nature does not like change. Religion means tradition and tradition is the anti-change. It is therefore understandable why so many people are opposed to changing anything in religion.

It is important to remember, however, that much of what we have today in religion, be it Christianity, Judaism, or Islam, was established several thousand years ago and all three religions were founded in the Middle East.

All three holy books, the Bible, the Torah, and the Quran, were drafted while taking current events of the time into consideration, such as health issues, social networks, laws and justice, finances, money lending and debts, the weather, and the geography of the land. To insist that some of the rulings cannot change to adapt the religion to modern times is unrealistic.

In Kazakhstan's case, one can see that happening, as far as the country's relationship with Islam is concerned, very clearly. While Kazakhstan is modernizing and adapting for Islam to fit in with its pace in a modern world, all while maintaining its traditions, a number of signs are starting to surface indicating that traditional Islam is making inroads in Kazakhstan.

For example, more and more car drivers are displaying sayings from the Quran or signs with the word "Allah" written in Arabic that hang from the rearview mirrors. How Kazakh drivers choose to decorate their cars may seem inconsequential and a small detail in the greater context of things, but small signs such as these can also take on a deeper meaning and give us an indication of approaching changes within a society. For the moment, say many Kazakhs, this is just a trend; it's not really religious, and it is nothing to worry about.

Almat Omirzaq, a scholar specializing in Arab affairs with the Kazakh Institute of Oriental Studies in Almaty, commented on this detail, pointing out the sign with the word "Allah" written in Arabic dangling from the taxi's mirror. Alluding to the driver, who was taking us to an appointment, Omirzaq said, "He probably drinks vodka and never goes to the mosque, but look at the sign on his mirror. Such decorations are becoming more and more common."

Kazakhstan the secular state wants very strongly to remain secular and has taken steps in the drafting of the constitution to make sure the country remains secular. One professor from the Eurasia University pointed out as we were walking through campus in Astana that every year she sees more and more women wearing not the veil, but headscarves.

And yet one more sign of the changing times: The cable television network of a friend in Almaty, Kazakhstan's largest city, replaced the BBC-TV network with a twenty-four-hour satellite channel broadcasting sayings from the Quran in Arabic.

What does this all mean? Does it mean that traditional Islam is winning the upper hand in Kazakhstan? Or does it mean that the Islamists are making progress ever so slowly? Or still, is it an indication that, yes, Islam and democracy can coexist?

Conclusion

"I believe in the fundamental Truth of all the great religions of the world. I believe that they are all God given. I came to the conclusion long ago . . . that all religions were true and also that all had some error in them."

—*Mahatma Gandhi*

One of the great lines in my all-time favorite movie, *Casablanca*, is when Rick, played by Humphrey Bogart, is asked by Capitaine Reynaud (Claude Raines) what brought him to Casablanca. "I came for the waters," replied Rick. "The waters? But we are in the middle of the desert," says Reynaud. "I was misinformed," shoots back Bogart with his inimitable sarcasm, knowing that his answers would fool no one.

Similarly, I was frequently asked when I first came to Astana in January 2010, in the dead of winter, what brought me to Astana. As if to make me feel better, most would add that it was the worst winter on record. Like Rick I replied, "I came for the waters."

When I arrived in Astana as a correspondent for the *Washington Times* I was the only foreign reporter in town; the few other foreign journalists covering Kazakhstan were based in the country's major city and former capital, Almaty. I wasn't exactly sure what I was in for, or even why the *Washington Times* had decided to set up a bureau in Kazakhstan while it was laying people off back in Washington. But that's another story.

I came to Kazakhstan with an open mind, although I must admit, I was slightly biased from some quick research before coming to Astana. Practically the only stories that appeared on the Internet about Kazakhstan were about human rights abuses and the government clamping down on the media. So I came prepared to be forced onto a flight back to the United States at a moment's notice.

With that in mind, one of the first stories I wrote upon arriving in Kazakhstan, after the one about Kazakhstan being awarded the chair of the OSCE, was about human rights abuses and the pressure placed on the local media by the government. I had intended to test the waters, so to speak. If the authorities didn't like my story I would be out of the country less than a week after my arrival.

The sole reaction from the authorities was that they made a point of mentioning that they had seen my story in the paper and that the minister read it—twice—and thought it was objective. Having marked my territory, I went about looking for the next angle to the story. What was it? From Washington it seemed to be that there was corruption in Kazakhstan on a monumental scale. Was there? Certainly, but that was not *the* story. There is corruption all over the world, starting right back at home on Capitol Hill. Just seek and ye shall find—if you know where to seek. Washington was excited about a story on prostitution in Kazakhstan. Are there prostitutes in Kazakhstan? Of course there are. Show me one country in the world where there are no prostitutes. Drive about two minutes from the *Washington Times* building in D.C. on New York Avenue at nine o'clock in the morning and you see more prostitutes than you do in Astana.

I started to meet foreign diplomats. In the course of the first month I was in Astana I met more than thirty ambassadors and probably an equal number of lower-ranking diplomats. From conversations at diplomatic functions and from talking to people, regular people and Kazakh officials, I began to realize that there was an untold story developing, and one that carried far more importance and would have far greater impact than a story on prostitutes—even one running tricks at $10,000 a shot on the high end, and $100 and less as advertised on a local website. The $10,000 lady of the night was pointed out to me in a club one night, and I was told she was the preferred belle of a politician.

Maybe there was a story there, but I doubted my editors would look kindly on an expense account that included a $10,000 "entertainment" line item. Rather, the story I found was the realization by a (mostly) Muslim country that something was wrong with Islam and that it had to be fixed quickly or it could grow like a malignant cancer and affect other healthier parts. That, and Kazakhstan's efforts to preempt Islamist terrorism. The government makes a point of simply calling it terrorism. For the Kazakhs, there cannot be any religion associated with a terrorist act. By resorting to terrorism the terrorists abandon their religion along the way.

But the government of President Nazarbayev recognizes that whatever terminology one uses does not change the facts. There are terrorist acts being carried out by Islamist extremists, and that issue has to be addressed. That, and the manner in which Kazakhstan approaches Islam, with such openness and easiness that is so different and refreshing from the way it is handled in so many other Muslim countries, is the story to be told.

There are major problems that need to be solved in the Muslim world and procrastination is a deadly disease that lures the best and brightest minds away from their countries of origin. These are serious problems that cannot and must not continuously be swept under the rug, as is often the case. Eventually, if the people most concerned by those problems do not act to address these issues accordingly, they are inviting disaster.

Reforms must be introduced before it is too late. The level of education must be enhanced in order to prepare the future generations who will lead their country. That task requires people with proper credentials. Women's and minorities' rights must be guaranteed in order to provide a safe and healthy environment for the people living in that country. The story as I saw it from Kazakhstan told me that this country was well on the way to establishing itself as a leader in the region. Coming out of Communism, I believed that this was the story to be told, and this is the story I hope this book will convey.

APPENDIX

An Interview with Nursultan Nazarbayev,
President of Kazakhstan

December 2010

CS: President Nazarbayev, a number of analysts believe that the West is waging war on Islam, and that this war was declared on September 11, 2001. I do not agree with such allegations for a variety of reasons. In my opinion, the problem is not the confrontation between Islam and the West, but within the Muslim world itself. Consequently, the solution should be sought there. If you were asked to find the solution, what steps would you take?

NN: As you know, we live in an era of globalization. One of its key aspects is rapprochement of various cultures. This process is inevitable. Therefore, we need to learn to get on well with each other. Mutual understanding is the key to peace and concord.

September 11, 2001, is the date of a serious shift in international politics. The entire world declared war on terrorism. I would like to stress that terrorism has no nationality or religious affiliation. This is an evil turned against humanity. I do not know any religion that encourages such activities. Terrorism is beyond religion, it is contrary to it.

Unfortunately, Islamophobia does exist. This happens primarily because of lack of knowledge. An average person perceives reality mostly through media and by communicating with others. These are not always reliable sources. Modern people are under the power of a form of the "intellectual idolatry," mentioned by Sir Francis Bacon.[1]

Meanwhile, Islam, like Christianity and Buddhism, is more than just a religion. It is a self-sufficient civilizational model. Think of Islamic banking and the halal industry.[2]

We know a lot of successful and peaceful countries where Islam is the state religion. They also are opposed to terrorism.[3]

Certainly, differences between the East and the West are significant. But precisely this diversity of cultures is the beauty and majesty of our world. This is not only my opinion, but also that of millions of citizens of my country.

Kazakhstan is a bridge between the East and the West. We are located in the heart of Eurasia. That is why since ancient times our land has been the crossroads of civilizations.

Today our country is home to 140 ethnicities and 46 faiths. Mosques, synagogues, and churches enjoy peaceful coexistence.

Every three years Astana hosts the Congresses of Leaders of World and Traditional Religions. Modern Kazakhstan is a place for constructive and friendly intercultural dialogue.

Efforts by both sides are crucial to achieving mutual understanding between [the] Islamic and Christian world.

States should do their best to counter the misuse of religious feelings for purposes of inciting conflicts. All social and political forces should actively participate in this respect. The stability of societies, states, regions, and beyond, that is directly related to the success of this process, as the security is indivisible.

Undoubtedly, every individual country needs its own approach to addressing interfaith discords. And the experience of Kazakhstan in this respect may certainly be an outstanding example to others.

CS: Do you see a certain analogy between Communism and radical Islam? Do you agree that just as Communism failed to pass the test of time and withstand the free will of the people, radical Islam is not eternal as well?

NN: The future is in hands of those who will be directed by constructive, moderate movements, those who will share the vision of peace and prosperity, believe in pluralism and seek to share [the] world's resources with others regardless of how they call God.

CS: Do you believe that over time the Islamist threat will finally disappear just as Communism dissipated in the Soviet Union?

NN: First of all, let me emphasize that I do not agree with the expression "Islamist threat." What we have here is the substitution of concepts. If a man dies for the idea, this does not mean that the idea is the truth. Even more so, a terrorist should not be considered as truly faithful. Islam and terrorism are not identical, but opposite concepts. Islam as such does not pose a threat. The danger comes from people who have distorted the understanding of faith.

For true Muslims, moral imperative is the moderation in all respects of the human life. Thus radicalism is not peculiar to Islam. Drawing a parallel between this religion and the USSR is not appropriate as well. The Soviet system is a social experiment artificially propagated against the will of most people.

As for Islam, it is, I repeat, a self-sufficient civilizational model. It has existed for over thirteen centuries, and has been developing naturally with an increasing number of followers.

In other words, Communism and Islam are categories that belong to different levels and planes. They aren't the same.

CS: Kazakhstan is a peaceful and quiet place where you can live undisturbed by the problems of the modern world, such as religious fanaticism and terrorism. Still, Kazakhstan does not give up its attempts to make our world better. You are chairing the OSCE. Next year you will be chairing the OIC. What is next?

NN: Chairmanship of the OSCE and OIC represents an opportunity to realize our ideas and share our vision of the world with the international community. By realizing our opportunities, we are not reducing but increasing their number, because one awakened idea awakes another.

We seek to make the world not just better but safer and more humane. The policies [of peaceful interfaith coexistence, education, and combating terrorism] conducted by Kazakhstan are a natural result of the events which have been occurring on our land.

In Soviet times, the Semipalatinsk Nuclear Test Site has been operating in Kazakhstan for half a century. It has conducted 456 nuclear and thermonuclear explosions. Their total capacity exceeded the power of the bomb dropped on Hiroshima by 2.5 thousand times.

Upon gaining independence, one of the first decrees I signed was to close down the test site. We also gave up the nuclear arms, which remained in our country. [With U.S. technical assistance the weapons were transported to the United States, where they were destroyed.] Moreover, at our initiative the whole of Central Asia became a nuclear-free zone.[4]

Kazakhstan has become a second home to millions of people of different ethnicities deported to our lands under the totalitarian regime. No matter how hard the Kazakh people were hit with misfortunes, they were always welcoming to all who sought shelter here.

Hospitality is the main law of the steppes, and it is in our blood.

When the USSR broke down, a number of Soviet republics were afflicted by ethnic conflicts. Kazakhstan has escaped this fate. Since early independence, we have managed to unite the society and implement the principle of the unity through diversity. We have established a unique institute, the People's Assembly of Kazakhstan, in order to ensure the protection of human rights and interests of all ethnic communities in our country.

Strengthening mutual understanding among nations and cultures is one of the priorities of our chairmanship of the OSCE.

Chairing the OIC will enable Kazakhstan to facilitate this process by promoting the ideals of a safe, predictable world, a world where there is no enmity between nations, where there is no nuclear threat, where all efforts of the states are aimed at creative direction.

CS: Today the world is concerned about religious terrorism. Despite the fact that Kazakhstan, fortunately, was not affected by this evil, it is a leader in the battle against it. In your opinion, how serious is the threat represented by this phenomenon?

NN: Indeed, Kazakhstan pays a particular attention to countering terrorism and related criminal activity—drug trafficking and illicit arms trafficking. We have joined all thirteen universal counterterrorism UN conventions.

I would like to stress again that terrorism does not belong to any nation or religion. It is the consequence of social and economic weakness of states and political instability. In such countries unlawful acts represent the only and permanent source of income. Therefore, if we want to eliminate terrorism, we should not rely only on military force. It is impossible to defeat international terrorism with military force alone. We should liquidate the factors promoting its development. Otherwise, year after year it will increase its capacity and threaten the global stability.

As of today, the main source of the key challenges of the modern world is Afghanistan. In this connection Kazakhstan renders considerable support. We have allocated $50 million for training of one thousand Afghan students in Kazakh higher education institutions. They can become familiar with the civic specialties and will see that it is possible to ensure well-being of the family without resorting to arms.

In addition, Kazakhstan assigned $4 million for restoration of schools, hospitals, and roads in Afghanistan. I am convinced that we need to more actively realize humanitarian initiatives in poor countries to defeat terrorism. It is necessary to promote reforms, both economic and political. We must give people education and faith in tomorrow, and show that it is possible to live without weapons in their hands.

CS: What is the religious situation in Kazakhstan? What is the role of religion in Kazakh society?

NN: You know, there is a saying: "The meaning of faith is not to settle in heaven, but to settle heaven in yourself." So today, in the twenty-first century, the main task of the state in the sphere of interfaith relations is that the citizens understand the textbook truth: all religions preach the ideals of peace, harmony, and unity.

The Communist, totalitarian political system of the Soviet era that was imposed upon Kazakhstan did not accept religion. The Soviet state was atheistic. With the collapse of Union, Kazakhstan experienced an economic depression and a shaky political system. People did not know what future awaited them. In this situation they just needed a spiritual support, they needed faith.

One of the first acts of the sovereign Kazakhstan was the law "On Freedom of Conscience and Religious Associations," adopted in 1992. Through successive stages of reform, we have created our own model of interethnic and interreligious harmony. Religious diversity is a sign of true religious tolerance of our people.

Since independence the number of religious communities increased sevenfold, and today they comprise almost 4,500. There are more than 3,300 mosques, churches, synagogues, and prayer houses in the country.

I also would like to note that in Kazakhstan, religious education extends to the secondary level [high school]. Permanent courses in the major mosques and Sunday schools at churches are functioning.

Given that Kazakhstan, according to the Constitution, is a secular state, the role of religion in society is large enough. It fulfills its true purpose: It helps people to live in peace and harmony with their neighbors.

As I said earlier, in our country the Congresses of Leaders of World and Traditional Religions are regularly held. Due to this, Kazakhstan became the center of interfaith dialogue and international integration. This important and responsible mission is a strategic vector of our state policy.

NOTES

Preface
1. Given that Arabic names and words are transliterated, there are often multiple spellings for the same word. The name of the Prophet is spelled as Mohamed, Mohamad, Muhamad, or Mohammad. Many Muslims never mention the Prophet's name without adding the words *S'al Allah aleyhi wasalam*. This roughly translates as "God's peace be upon him."
2. The same holds for the Quran (Koran). Muslims will quite frequently follow the word "Quran" with the word *karim*, meaning "holy."
3. *Salafi* denotes a follower of a Sunni Islamist movement that takes the pious predecessors, the *Salaf* of the patristic period of early Islam, as exemplary models. The word *Salaf* in Arabic can be interpreted as "ancestor." *Salafis* tend to use a stricter interpretation of scripture. The movement has become prominent since 1803.
4. *Takfiris* are typically a violent offshoot of the *Salafi* movement, the difference being that while *Salafis* are often described as "fundamentalist Muslims" or "Islamists," it is not necessarily a violent movement and does not support terrorists. *Takfiris* on the other hand have turned to violence as a tool, which they see as being legitimate in their jihad in order to achieve their political or religious goals. *Takfiris* reject any change in Islam as it was revealed to the Prophet.

Chapter 1: Islam Without a Veil
1. Armenia, Azerbaijan, Belarus, Estonia, Georgia, Kazakhstan, Kyrgyzstan, Latvia, Lithuania, Moldova, Russia, Tajikistan, Turkmenistan, Ukraine, and Uzbekistan.

2. *Ijtihad* is the institutionalized practice of interpreting Islamic law (sharia) to take into account changing historical circumstances, and, therefore, it brings about the possibility of different views.
3. A fundamentalist does not necessarily have to be an extremist. Many are those who mistakenly call Islamists fundamentalists.

Chapter 2: Islamophobia
1. Sam Harris, "Bombing our Illusion," *Huffington Post*, October 10, 2005. The idea that Islam is a "peaceful religion hijacked by extremists" is now a particularly dangerous fantasy for moderate Muslims to indulge.
2. Javed Mohammed, *Islam 101: Ultimate Guide to Understanding Islam.* (Milpitas, CA: Pyramid Connections, 2003), 6.
3. Ibid., 7.
4. David Smock, "*Ijtihad*: Reinterpreting Islamic Principles for the Twenty-First Century." The United States Institute of Peace and the Center for the Study of Islam and Democracy, August 2004, 1–7.
5. Akbar S. Ahmed, *Islam Under Siege.* (Cambridge, UK: Polity, 2003), 1.
6. John L. Esposito, ed., *Political Islam: Revolution, Radicalism, or Reform?* (Boulder, CO: Lynne Rienner Publishers, 1997), 1.
7. Ahmed, *Islam Under Siege*, 7.
8. Ibid., 105.
9. Mohammed, *Islam 101*, 7.

Chapter 3: Kazakhstan Emerges
1. From an e-mail sent to the author in July 2010.

Chapter 4: The New End Game in Central Asia
1. Ambassador Pierre Morel, special European envoy to Central Asia. Panel at Johns Hopkins School of Advanced International Studies in Washington, D.C., September 23, 2010.
2. Conference held at the United States Institute of Peace on the topic of *Ijtihad*, Washington, D.C., March 19, 2004.
3. Edward Schatz, "The Politics of Multiple Identities: Lineage and Ethnicity in Kazakhstan." *Europe-Asia Studies*, May 2000, 489.
4. Kanat Saudabayev, foreign minister of Kazakhstan. "Remarks on Reducing Nuclear Dangers, Increasing Global Security." These remarks were made at a symposium held on December 16, 2003, at the Dirksen Senate Office Building of the U.S. Senate. At that point, Kanat Saudabayev was Kazakhstan's ambassador to the United States.

5. Ibid.
6. Claude Salhani, *While the Arab World Slept: The Impact of the Bush Years on the Middle East* (Washington, DC: Middle East Politics & Policies, September 2009), 23.

Chapter 5: The "Kazakhi" Way: Economy First, Politics Second

1. John L. Esposito, ed., *Political Islam: Revolution, Radicalism, or Reform?* (Boulder, CO: Lynne Rienner Publishers, 1997), 3.
2. Ibid., 23.
3. Remarks by Imam Hassan Qawzini at workshop titled "Ijtihad: Reinterpreting Islamic Principles for the Twenty-first Century," cosponsored by the United States Institute of Peace and the Center for the Study of Islam and Democracy, Washington, DC, March 19, 2004.
4. Claude Salhani, "Scourge of 'Islam Experts,'" Islamicity.com, http://www.islamicity.com/articles/Articles.asp?ref=IV1001-4059.
5. The United States Institute of Peace and the Center for the Study of Islam and Democracy cosponsored a workshop on *Ijtihad* in March 2004.
6. Claude Salhani, "Opening the Gates of *Ijtihad*," Search for Common Ground News Service, March 7, 2006, http://www.acommongroundnews.org/article.php?id=2579&lan=en&sid=1&sp=1.
7. Pat Langa, "The Gate of *Ijtihad*," *Washington Times*, March 11, 2006, 12.
8. David Smock, "*Ijtihad*," 1-7 USIP 2004 Report.
9. Ibid.
10. Salhani, "Opening the Gates of *Ijtihad*."

Chapter 6: Shaking Things Up

1. According to the "Islamic Scholar," a comprehensive CD-ROM of all issues relating to Islam.
2. Madrassa is the Arabic word for school.
3. The plural of *talib* is *taliban*.
4. John Esposito and Dalia Mogahed, *Who Speaks for Islam? What a Billion Muslims Really Think* (New York: Gallup Press, 2007), 88.
5. More recently, many secular Turks feel that the government of current prime minster Recep Tayyip Erdogan and his ruling Justice and Development Party (AKP) are taking the country away from the staunchly secular system of government put in place by Atatürk, the founder of modern-day Turkey. Erdogan is an Islamist, as is his party.

6. Kazakhstan shares a water border with Iran on the Caspian Sea.

7. Kazakhstan borders Turkmenistan and Uzbekistan, which in turn border Afghanistan.

8. Other Muslim countries have a combination of sharia and either English or French law, depending on which country colonized them.

9. "Culture of Kazakhstan," *Wikipedia*, last modified March 21, 2011, http://en.wikipedia.org/wiki/Culture_of_Kazakhstan.

10. Every country has a chief mufti who speaks on behalf of his community and represents the Sunni branch of Islam in his country, but unlike the hierarchy in Shiism or in Christian churches, the mufti does not hold the same power.

11. 2009 estimate.

12. Conseil Français du Culte Musulman.

13. Shamanism includes the belief that those who practice it, Shamans, act as messengers between the spiritual and human worlds. They are said to be able to treat illness and various ailments by "mending the soul."

14. Tangri or Tengri refers to an ancient Turkic celestial being.

15. Zoroastrianism is a religion and philosophy based on the teachings of the prophet Zoroaster (also known as Zarathustra).

16. Nestorianism is a Christological doctrine advanced by the patriarch of Constantinople in AD 428, Nestorius. The doctrine along with its author was declared heretical, because he emphasized the disunion between the human and divine natures of Jesus.

Chapter 7: The Road to Moderation

1. Ludwig von Bertalanffy's General Systems Theory (GST) assumes that everything and everyone is part of a system. Some can belong to more than one system. For example, one can be a certain nationality, thus belonging to the nation's system. But at the same time if that person belongs to a certain religion, they can also belong to that system. Additionally, that same person will belong to his or her family system, and so on. Von Bertalanffy theorizes that any change to the system brings conflict, as the system has to open up to allow the new part to join, or it has to reject it. Some conflict can be beneficial to the system, but the fact remains that change disturbs the system.

2. Kazakhstan borders Russia, China, Kyrgyzstan, Uzbekistan, and Turkmenistan, and it has water borders through the Caspian Sea with Iran and Azerbaijan.

Chapter 8: Islam and Modernization
1. M. R. Bawai Muhaiyaddeen, *Islam and World Peace: Explanations of a Sufi* (Philadelphia, PA: Fellowship Press, 1987, 2007), 89.

Chapter 9: The Kazakhstan Experiment
1. Discussion held at the Johns Hopkins School of Advanced International Studies in Washington, DC, September 25, 2010.

Chapter 10: The Terror Threat and Reasons for Concern
1. Martha Brill Olcott, "The War on Terrorism in Central Asia and Cause of Democratic Reform," http://www.carnegieendowment.org/publications/index.cfm?fa=view&id=1320, accessed September 1, 2010.
2. Ibid.
3. The war on terror always struck me as an odd choice of words, because terror is an emotion, like fear or hate. Therefore, the war on terrorism seems more correct.
4. Al-Ikhwan al-Muslimun is the Arabic name for the Muslim Brotherhood.
5. The sayings and living habits of the Prophet.
6. In 1981 Syrian President Hafez al-Assad ordered his army to surround the Syrian city of Hama where the Brotherhood had retrenched, and commanded his troops to use artillery to practically level the city.
7. The Islamic Group.
8. Excommunication and Migration.
9. Qutb wrote *Milestones,* one of the most influential books in Islamist literature.
10. The Lincoln Brigade was composed of Americans who joined up on the side of the Republicans in the Spanish Civil War to fight against the Fascists.
11. CNN special investigation dated January 6, 2010.

Chapter 12: Can Democracy and Islam Coexist?
1. Private interview granted to the author on October 21, 2010, in Astana.
2. According to figures from the U.S. Department of State.
3. The Levant usually includes the countries of the Eastern Mediterranean basin: Syria, Lebanon, Palestine, Israel, and trans-Jordan, today called Jordan.
4. The Hijaz was a province of the Ottoman Empire in what is now Saudi Arabia.
5. Nur Otan ("The Light of Fatherland" in Kazakh); Azat ("Free," formerly known as True AkZhol); the National Social Democratic Party; AkZhol ("Bright Path"); Auyl ("Farm"); the Communist Party of Kazakhstan;

the Communist People's Party; Party of Patriots; Adilet ("Justice"); and Rukhaniyat ("Spirituality").

Chapter 13: A Conversation with a Salafi

1. The acronym INRI that often appear just above the head of Jesus on crucifixes stands for Jesus of Nazareth, King of the Jews. Or, in Latin, Iesus Nazarenus, Rex Iudaeorum.
2. New Oxford American Dictionary.
3. All that is needed to convert to Islam is for someone to recite the words of the *Shahada*.
4. *Kalima* means "Word."
5. M. R. Bawa Muhaiyaddeen, *Islam and World Peace: Explanations of a Sufi* (Philadelphia, PA: Fellowship Press, 1987, 2007), 62.
6. Ibid.
7. A traditional Islamic term for Christians, which literally means the "Nazarene." Arab Christians never use that word to refer to themselves, because it tends to have a negative connotation.
8. Alex DiBranco, "Hundreds of Uzbek Women Report Forced Sterilization," Change.org, July 20, 2010, http://news.change.org/stories/hundreds-of-uzbek-women-report-forced-sterilization.
9. Egyptian president Gamal Abdel Nasser (1918–1970), officially the second president of Egypt, was the instigator of the Egyptian Revolution of July 1952, a bloodless coup that overthrew the monarchy of King Farouk, turned Egypt into an Arab republic, and launched a popular pan-Arab movement that saw in him a great unifier in the Arab world. His policies were in fact disastrous.
10. Houari Boumediène, (1927–1978). Leader of the Algerian revolution and later president of Algeria. His Front de Libération Nationale forced France out of what was considered an integral part of France. Algeria was not a colony, but it consisted of two French departments. He became a popular figure in the Arab World.
11. Michel Aflaq (1910–1989) and Salah al-Bitar (1912–1980) are the co-founders of the Baath Party. The Baath Party continued to exist after the deaths of its founders but underwent a great split, with one faction becoming the Syrian Baath and the other the Iraqi Baath.

Chapter 15: Changin' Times

1. John L. Esposito, *Islam: The Straight Path* (New York: Oxford University Press, 2005), 79.

2. John L. Esposito, *Unholy War: Terror in the Name of Islam* (Oxford, UK: Oxford University Press, 2002), 30.
3. According to the New Oxford Dictionary.
4. Bernard Lewis, "Islamic Revolution," *New York Review of Books*, January 21, 1988, http://www.nybooks.com/articles/4557.

Appendix: An Interview with Nursultan Nazarbayev, President of Kazakhstan

1. Sir Francis Bacon argued that human folly arose from a virtual enslavement of the mind to intellectual idolatry. He pointed out four "idols": 1. Idols of the tribe have their foundation in human nature itself. 2. Idols of the cave concern common errors of the individual's nature. 3. Idols of the marketplace arise from consort, intercourse, commerce. 4. Idols of the theater refer to dogmatic belief in sensory illusions.
2. Both the Islamic banking system and the halal industry, where meats have to be treated in a certain way and under the guidance of a religious figure (not unlike kosher foods), are flourishing industries.
3. Jordan, Morocco, Qatar, Bahrain, United Arab Emirates, Kuwait, Oman, and others.
4. As mentioned previously, at the breakup of the USSR Kazakhstan was the fourth-largest nuclear power. It got rid of all the weapons.

BIBLIOGRAPHY AND
SUGGESTED READING

Ahmed, Akbar S. *Islam Under Siege: Living Dangerously in a Post-Honor World*. Cambridge, UK: Polity Press, 2003.

Braswell Jr., George W. *What You Need to Know About Islam & Muslims*. Nashville, TN: Broadman & Holman, 2000.

Cooley, John. *Unholy Wars: Afghanistan, America and International Terrorism*. Third Edition. Sterling, VA: Pluto Press, 2002.

Esack, Farid. *Qur'an Liberation & Pluralism: An Islamic Perspective of Interreligious Solidarity Against Oppression*. Oxford, UK: One World Publications, 2002.

Esposito, John L., ed. *Political Islam: Revolution, Radicalism, or Reform?* Boulder, CO: Lynne Rienner Publishers, 1997.

Esposito, John L., and Dalia Mogahed. *Who Speaks for Islam?: What a Billion Muslims Really Think*. New York: Gallup Press, 2007.

El Fadl, Khaled Abou. *Islam and the Challenge of Democracy*. Princeton, NJ: Princeton University Press, 2004.

Gerecht, Reuel Marc. *The Islamic Paradox: Shiite Clerics, Sunni Fundamentalists, and the Coming of Arab Democracy*. Washington, D.C.: AEI Press, 2004.

Gordon, Philip H., and Omer Taspinar. *Winning Turkey: How America, Europe, and Turkey Can Revive a Fading Partnership*. Washington, D.C.: Brookings Institution Press, 2008.

Jafarzadeh, Alireza. *The Iran Threat: President Ahmadinejad and the Coming Nuclear Crisis*. New York: Palgrave Macmillan, 2007.

Javed, Mohammed. *Islam 101: Ultimate Guide to Understanding Islam*. Milpitas, CA: Pyramid Connections, 2003.

Kuftaro, Sheikh Ahmad. *The Way of Truth*. Damascus, Syria: no publisher, no date.

Manji, Irshad. *The Trouble with Islam: A Muslim's Call for Reform in Her Faith*. New York: St. Martin's Press, 2003.

Muasher, Marwan. *The Arab Center: The Promise of Moderation*. New Haven: Yale University Press, 2008.

Muhaiyaddeen, M. R. Bawa. *Islam & World Peace*. Philadelphia, PA: Fellowship Press, 1987, 2007.

Rauf, Imam Feisal Abdul. *What's Right with Islam: A New Vision for Muslims and the West*. San Francisco: HarperSanFrancisco, 2004.

Salhani, Claude. *While the Arab World Slept: The Impact of the Bush Years on the Middle East*. Washington, D.C.: Middle East Politics & Policies, September 2009.

Schatz, Edward. "The Politics of Multiple Identities: Lineage and Ethnicity in Kazakhstan." *Europe-Asia Studies*, 2000.

Schwartz, Stephen. *The Other Islam: Sufism and the Road to Global Harmony*. New York: Doubleday, 2008.

Taras, Raymond C., and Rajat Ganguly. *Understanding Ethnic Conflict: The International Dimension*. New York: Longman, 2002.

Thier, J. Alexander, ed. *The Future of Afghanistan*. Washington, D.C.: United States Institute of Peace, 2009.

Warraq, Ibn, ed. *Leaving Islam: Apostates Speak Out*. Amherst, NY: Prometheus Books, 2003.

INDEX

Index 201

Muslim Brotherhood, 6, 119, 131, 133, 164, 165, 193
Muslimness, 80, 81
Mustafa Kemal. *See* Atatürk

Nanay, Julia, 51
NATO, 48, 60, 150, 153
Nazarbayev, Nursultan, 18–19, 23, 26, 33, 35, 54–56, 74–83, 93, 107–108, 112–113, 122–123, 145, 149–156, 164, 168, 181, 183
"near beyond," 44, 48, 49
Nietzsche, Friedrich, 93
niqab, 81
North Korea, 77, 105
Nur Otan Party, 80

OIC, 27, 28, 84, 89, 94, 97, 115, 185, 186
oil, 2, 44, 47, 48, 49, 51, 104, 108, 109, 117, 122, 135, 149, 170
Olcott, Martha Brill, 126, 193
Organization for Security and Cooperation in Europe. *See* OSCE
Organization of Islamic Conference. *See* OIC
OSCE, 18, 19, 27, 33, 40, 41, 83, 97, 105, 107, 108, 109, 115, 116, 137, 150, 181
Ottoman Empire, 76, 79, 152, 194

Palestine Liberation Organization, 133
Pasquino, Bruno Antonio, 26, 32
Peat, Tomash, 62
Perl, Raphael, 83
PFC Energy, 51

Qawzini, Hassan, 61, 68, 90, 91
Quran, 13, 16, 27–28, 33, 46, 64–65, 74, 76, 131, 147, 158, 160–162, 177–178, 189

Reagan, Ronald, 1, 2, 8, 88, 155
Red Brigades, 134
religion, 5, 9, 10, 13, 14, 16, 18, 19, 23, 25, 26, 27, 28, 32, 33, 36, 37, 38, 47, 48, 52, 57, 58, 61, 62, 63, 64, 65, 66, 72, 73, 76, 77, 78, 79, 80, 81, 82, 84, 87, 88, 90, 92, 94, 95, 96, 99, 100,
102, 103, 104, 105, 106, 107, 109, 111, 112, 113, 114, 117, 125, 127, 144, 146, 150, 151, 152, 153, 155, 158, 159, 161, 162, 163, 164, 165, 168, 170, 174, 175, 176, 177, 182

Salafi, 69, 71, 73–74, 87, 100, 106, 112, 129, 157–159, 161–163, 165, 175, 189, 194
Sarkozy, Nicolas, 47, 83
Schatz, Edward, 42, 190
Shabab, 119
Siddiqi, Muzammil H, 68
Stalin, Josef, 6, 41
Star Wars. *See* Strategic Defense Initiative
Sting, 77
Strategic Defense Initiative, 2
Sultanov, Bulat, 37, 58

Takfiri, 37, 45, 66, 69, 71, 79, 83, 85, 91, 99, 106, 115, 129, 136, 161, 162, 176, 189
Takir wal Hijra, 132
Taliban, 18, 21, 46–47, 78, 79, 99, 106, 113, 115–116, 118–119, 121, 128
terrorism, 14, 16, 48, 58, 66, 77, 83, 88–89, 92, 97, 99, 104–105, 107, 113, 119, 121, 125 128, 130–138, 141–145, 148, 151, 166, 181, 183–187, 193
Turkmenistan, 9, 25, 34, 47, 106, 109, 122, 189, 192

United States Institute of Peace, 64, 67, 190, 191
Uzbekistan, 9, 22, 25, 34, 36, 47, 85, 106, 109, 111, 114, 115, 118, 122, 126, 129, 138, 163, 189, 192

Vashadze, Grigol, 40
Vickers, Michael, 121

war on terror, 130, 193
Washington Times, 26
weapons, 2, 22, 38, 42, 43, 105, 107, 112, 118, 151, 168, 170, 186, 187, 197
WMD, 42, 43

Yusef, 157–162

ABOUT THE AUTHOR

C laude Salhani is a political analyst specializing in the Middle East, politicized Islam, and terrorism. He just completed a six-month assignment for the *Washington Times* in Astana, the capital of Kazakhstan, during which time he interviewed the country's top leaders and accompanied the foreign minister on his travels in the region. This is his first book on Central Asia.

Salhani is a senior associate with the Institute of World Affairs and a member of the London-based International Institute for Strategic Studies. He appears regularly on a number of television programs as a political commentator, and he speaks English, French, Italian, Spanish, and Arabic. Over the course of his thirty-year career as a journalist, Mr. Salhani has traveled to eighty-three countries, covered twelve wars, was wounded in battle three times, and was nominated for a Pulitzer Prize for his coverage of the U.S. Marines in Lebanon.

His articles have appeared in the *New York Times*, the *International Herald Tribune*, the *Washington Times*, the *Times* (London), the *San Francisco Chronicle*, the *San Diego Union Tribune*, and numerous journals.

Mr. Salhani's recent books include *Black September to Desert Storm* (University of Missouri Press, 1987) and *While the Arab World Slept: The Impact of the Bush Years on the Middle East* (Middle East Politics & Policies, 2009), and he is a contributing author of *The Iraq War* (Brassey's, 2004) and *Terrorism & the Media* (Oxford Press, forthcoming).